SUBIC

An Epochal Philippine Town the U.S. Navy Helped Shape

Angel N. Pagaduan

PublishAmerica
Baltimore

© 2007 by Angel N. Pagaduan.

All rights reserved. No part of this book may be reproduced, stored in a retrieval system or transmitted in any form or by any means without the prior written permission of the publishers, except by a reviewer who may quote brief passages in a review to be printed in a newspaper, magazine or journal.

First printing

ISBN: 1-4241-8277-8
PUBLISHED BY PUBLISHAMERICA, LLLP
www.publishamerica.com
Baltimore

Printed in the United States of America

**Available @ ARKIPELAGO Books
1010 Mission Street
San Francisco, CA 94103 USA
www.arkipelagobooks.com**

DEDICATION

This book is dedicated to the people of Subic and to others who have heard about or are familiar with the town, mere mention of which—to people almost anywhere—often conjures up nostalgic reminiscences of the exotic, a once-famed Subic Bay U.S. Naval facility complex, or a world-class tourism-sojourning interest.

It is dedicated more particularly to a pre-composed critique team of Subiqeunian professional educators who subjected it to a sentence-by-sentence validating scrutiny, head of whom is Dr. Amelia Hebron Mojica, Ed. D., Subic Department of Education District Supervisor, with the participation as members of Merlina Pasion Cruz, Ph. D., Principal I, Ilwas Elementary School, and Josephine F. Khonghun, Special Education Center for the Gifted; Clarita Cleto Adolfo-Lagrama*, Master Teacher II, Subic Central School; and Bernadette Odias Sandoval*, Master Teacher II, Josephine F. Khonghun Special Education Center for the Gifted.

*Both are Subic-born professional educators

ACKNOWLEDGMENTS

The persons named hereunder are due special thanks:

For permission for referential use of their *Subic Through the Years* research book that was sponsored and funded by the Subic municipal government in 1998:

Esther F. Dimalanta—Santo Tomas Elementary School teacher
Lino F. Mercado—Subic National High School teacher
Lydia E. Solomon—Calapacuan Elementary School principal (retired)

For their encouragement in 2006-2007, in the writing of the book as a historical and educational undertaking:

Sequel Albano—Retired Subic Bay U.S. Naval Base employee now living in California
Sr. Rosa C. Mendoza—Saint James School principal
Dr. Felita C. Pullido, Ed. D.—Subic National High School principal
Myrla Raymundo—Past employee of the Subic Bay U.S. Naval Base now living in California and serving as Alameda County Commissioner, Union City Historical Museum founder/CEO/Newsletter editor, and Friends of Union City Library President
Atty. Romulo M. Villamil—Lawyer interchangeably living in Dagupan City and California (he was a past consul general of the Philippine Consular Office at San Francisco)

For their invaluable help for confirmative checking of the book's facts and figures pertinently relating to Olongapo as once a Subic barrio:

Vic Flores Bizcocho—Public Information-Press Relations Officer, Olongapo City
Delfin Juico, Jr.—Secretary, Olongapo City Mayor's Office

For their invaluable help in identifying/confirming Subiquenos who had joined with the U.S. Navy, as well as Subiqeunas who got married to USN sailors:

Cristina (Neneng) Ramos de Jesus—Native Subiquenian residing in Union City, California

Eliseo (Ely) Labampa—Retiree, Subic U.S. Naval Base and now California resident

Franco Del Monte—Past US Navy servicemen and part-time realitor

Contents

CHAPTER 1	9
A GEM OF GEOGRAPHICAL ASSET	10
MUNICIPALITY'S POPULATION	16
CULTURE	18
MUNICIPAL ECONOMY	42
MUNICIPAL GOVERNMENT AND POLITICS	51
A Classic Fruition of Political Adventure	58
CHAPTER 2	60
SALIENT FEATURES OTHER THAN THE FAMOUS SUBIC BAY	60
CHAPTER 3	63
EARLY WAYS OF LIFE	63
CHAPTER 4	67
CHAPTER 5	78
ONSET OF U.S. EMERGENCE	79
SUBIC AS A WAR ZONE	82
FIRST PHASE OF U.S. RULE, 1898-1935	85
THE COMMONWEALTH PERIOD OF U.S. RULE, 1935-41	88
CHAPTER 6	98
OCCUPATION OF SUBIC	99
INCEPTION OF CIVILIAN (PUPPET) GOVERNMENT	117
ADAPTATIONS TO WARTIME'S RESTRAINTS ON COMMUNITY LIVING	126
BIRTH AND OPERATIONS OF THE SUBIC UNDERGROUND RESISTANCE	129
CHAPTER 7	143
SIDE OPERATIONS IN SUBDUING AN ENEMY ON THE DEFENSE	144
LIBERATION'S IMMEDIATE AFTER-EFFECTS	147
CHAPTER 8	154
MAJOR EVENTS IN THE WAKE OF JAPAN'S SURRENDER	155
POST-INDEPENDENCE EVENTS OF FAR-REACHING SIGNIFICANCE	158
CHAPTER 9	167
SUBICQUENIANS IN PEDESTALS OF ILLUSTRIOUSNESS IN THE U.S.	168

CHAPTER 10	172
APPENDIX A	181
APPENDIX B	183
APPENDIX C	186
APPENDIX D	188
APPENDIX E	189
APPENDIX F	191
APPENDIX G	193
APPENDIX H	195
APPENDIX I	196

1

New and Old Subic in Glimpses

From a once common-looking, third class municipality in the province of Zambales, the town of Subic today shows a striking new look: wide-spread socio-economic advancement manifested with tangible progress and modernity. As a town that mothered Zambales' first city, Olongapo, a past barrio made into a metropolis by a Subic-based segment of the U.S. Navy, it in fact is expected to metamorphose, too, in the near future from a first-class municipality into a city—Zambales' second. Its growing population and income as generally reflected in multiplying homes of common to remarkable styles, businesses of various kinds including dealerships in computers and cell phones, and public and private structures of larger dimensions, not to mention concrete roads that were predominantly dirt roads in the past, particularly attracts travelers' attention. Equally striking is a new sight, too, in the now fully air-conditioned Subic Municipal Hall: an aura of dignified service professionalism exercised by impressively uniformed officials and the rank-and-file—all identifiable by their chest-worn IDs. Indeed, scenarios of officials' infrequent accessibility and of staff expenditure of time for anything but work have become a thing of the past.

These are concrete indicators of contemporary conditions in Subic that make it an apt and timely focus of a town study geared objectively for a perspective view of its history.

A GEM OF GEOGRAPHICAL ASSET

Subic Bay

As Zambales's northward gateway town from the direction of Manila, capital of the Philippines, Subic has become one of the Orient's favorite tourist spots. It became renowned worldwide largely because of its most important geographical attribute: Subic Bay—an inlet of the Pacific Ocean that washes scenically at the town's picturesque coasts with dainty, frolicsome beaches. It happens to have a multi-utilitarian value, and this stems from its ideal conditions for fishing, milkfish farming, swimming, beach partying, and harbor purposes. Sea-sports-based enterprises, including SCUBA diving and beach resort entrepreneurships proliferated in it with the onset of modernity. Not frequented by deadly sharks, nature's endowment of its placid, mild-degreed water, enhanced by the added joy of sun-kissed and sea-breezed sojourns in world-class hotels, makes for its irresistible charm to both domestic and international tourists. It is apparently for this reason that Subic Bay was chosen for a past economic summit of world leaders that included no less than U.S. President Bill Clinton. That multimedia-monitored gathering of a global group of top political minds was held within the environmentally clean, well-kept, indoor-outdoor accommodations of the Subic Bay Metropolitan Authority (SBMA) complex as "progenitored" by the once-famed Subic Bay U.S. Naval Base—its precursor. But more significantly, it is Subic Bay's natural endowment of a strategic location and configuration that assays its greatest value: a geographical gem of sinew for pillaring an economy.

The first to harbor this notion was Juan de Salcedo, grandson of Miguel Lopez de Legazpe, first Spanish settler of Cebu, during Spain's colonial venture into the Philippines. In 1572, he reported on Subic Bay's good features: "deep water, sheltered anchorages, and strategic location." Subsequent to this, a Spanish Naval Commission ordered, on March 8, 1885, the construction of a naval arsenal in Olongapo, then originally a Subic barrio. But the Spanish-U.S. war broke out in 1898. When an armistice was signed in Paris on December 10 of the same year, it provided for Spain's freeing of Cuba and ceding—to the U.S.—Puerto Rico, Guam, and the Philippines. When the U.S. took over Spain's control of the Philippines, Spain got paid $20 million from the U.S. This impinged on the sensibilities of Filipinos, but exactly one year after the Treaty of Paris was signed, on December 10, 1899, use of the originally Spanish-built Subic Bay naval fortification transferred to the U.S.

Subic Bay became the site of a number of sudden disruptions. Some forty years later, or on December 7, 1941, the Empire of Japan's navy launched a sneak attack on Pearl Harbor, a U.S. Naval Base in Hawaii. Practically on the same day (but already December 8 in the Philippines), Japanese planes also bombed, without warning, the Subic Bay U.S. Naval Base in Olongapo, not to mention other places in the Subic town itself. These acts precipitated entry of the U.S. into World War II, and Japan's "day of infamy." The war ultimately saw the U.S. as the victor. Japan unconditionally surrendered on September 2, 1945—an inevitable aftermath of the awesomeness of the most destructive war weapon the world had ever seen: the atomic bomb. The Subic Bay U.S. Naval Base was, thenceforth, relied on as democracy's bulwark of freedom, the largest post-World War II ship repair facility of the U.S. off continental America. The reconditioned Subic Bay U.S. Naval Base served to ensure peace—right when the grim dangers of the Cold War imminently threatened to break it any moment. But time ultimately proved somehow providential in seeing where and how Subic stands today—economically and socially.

Subic Bay U.S. Naval Base's Legacy

To Filipinos, the word "barrio" ordinarily means a town's residential area that was rural-looking or less urban in aura than the town itself. But the former barrio, Olongapo, was a distinctively particular exception. Even before World War II, Olongapo—not Subic—was already a busy hub or an urbanized center for jobs, businesses, recreation, cinematic entertainment, and other community activities. The national holiday, Rizal Day, honoring Dr. Jose Rizal, the Philippines' foremost national hero, was annually celebrated more festively in Olongapo—right within the Subic Bay U.S. Naval Base reservation area. Held during the Christmas season, it was punctuated with one of the event's most popular, crowd-attracting activity: the handing out to children of various American gifts for the Yuletide. It was largely for this reason that parents from Subic town were wont to go to its 10-kilometer-distant Olongapo barrio with children in tow every Rizal Day. And for movies, it was also to Olongapo that Subic folks traveled to see pre-chosen films shown at either of the place's only two theatres of the era: Cine Naval and Cine Oriental.

In sum, the whole scenario is seen rooted to Olongapo's being the site where the Subic Bay U.S. Naval Base was established because of its being strategically encompassed within the bounds of Subic Bay.

Olongapo was made a city and separated from the Subic municipality in the mid-1960s through a law authored by the Zambales Congressman Ramon Magsaysay, Jr., now one of the stalwarts of the Philippine senate. This was done in light of a significant growth in its population and income— a result of the Subic Bay U.S. Naval Base's decades-long operations in Subic. In an interview, Efren Mendigorin, Subic CATV manager, claimed to have a copy of the record or charter for Olongapo's conversion into Zambales' first city.

When the Military Bases Agreement ended on September 16, 1991, most Filipinos, particularly in Subic, preferred that the U.S. Navy stays. There were two principal reasons for this. One was that its pullout portended termination of job opportunities that provided good pay and fringe benefits enjoyed by a countrywide-sourced workforce. The other arose from concerns that—as what later actually happened with the Clark Air Base—pilferage would thin out the assets that would be left behind.

But actual pullout results proved otherwise for the second reason. What instead emerged in the void left in the wake of the pull-out of the U.S. Navy was the Subic Bay Metropolitan Authority (SBMA)—primed into a new entity that preserved existing assets and infrastructure in generally pristine condition. It has since been serving the multinational business operations of various revenue-raising categories it runs on today. The SBMA became what it presently is only because of thousands of civic-minded citizens' demonstration of a timeless Filipino tradition: bayanihan, or spirit of volunteerism. They went out of their way to labor to make the SBMA a reality—even without immediate pay. This was made possible under the leadership of the then Olongapo City Mayor Richard J. Gordon in his capacity as founding SBMA chairman—a post that later saw him elected senator of the Philippines.

Legacy's Long-Range Socioeconomic Impact

From the standpoint of local, provincial, and national economic interests, the SBMA today is functioning like a heavy-duty generator of financial power seen as being vital to development. In the minds of many, this had come about largely because of—as veritably an epochal legacy—the U.S. Navy's stay of many years in Subic. Incidentally, this sees a parallel benefit in the fact that countless laid-off civilian employees following the U.S. Naval Base's phase-out, not to count earlier retirees, gained special U.S. immigrant visas. (Appendix A shows some retirees known to have been accordingly benefited.) By the same token, many of Subic's youth, as well as others from elsewhere in the Philippines, got inducted into the U.S. Navy as early as 1945, when U.S. General Douglas MacArthur and the forces under his command liberated the Philippines from Japanese hands. Qualified Subic youths' induction into the U.S. Navy was effected mainly at a submarine base that was exigently built in early 1945 in Agusuhin—a seaside portion of a huge mountain towering over Subic town—by a USN construction battalion called "Sea Bees." Located just about 7 miles from the main Subic Bay U.S. Naval Base in Olongapo, then newly freed from Japanese control, that submarine base became defunct after Japan's surrender to the U.S. on September 1945. This notwithstanding, many young Filipinos, particularly in Subic, continued to seek induction into the U.S. Navy through the years, and this was right through its improved Subic Bay Naval Base in Olongapo. Appendix B shows a list of Subiquenian youths known to have joined with the U.S. Navy as pioneers, and succeeding inductees.

How this impacted the life of those who later got honorably retired is best shown, partly or wholly, by the fact that many of the stylish homes in Subic today belong to retired USN sailors, mostly Filipinos, but also some Americans. Some had established dual residence—one in Subic and another in the U.S. for alternate vacations in and between the two places. On the whole, though, more retirees live permanently in the U.S., but some retain accommodations for their once-in-a-while vacation in Subic.

Many women who got married to USN sailors eventually earned U.S. citizenship. This situation has inevitably resulted in many Subic citizens' immigration to the U.S. via petitions by their U.S.-domiciled relatives—husband, wife, son, daughter, brother, etc. Because of the higher standard of living, many past Subic citizens now find themselves established permanently in the U.S. despite having across-the-seas domiciles. By this account, the proportion of original family or household members to newcomers from the present generation in Subic has shrunk considerably over the years.

Financial Security and Love Quest in USN Sailors' Ubiquity in Subic

In the course of the U.S. Navy's stay in Subic, its sailors, regardless of ethnicity, gained the reputation of being looked up to, particularly for their being blessed with fat dollar-to-peso pockets plus exclusive PX privileges, other considerations put aside. This understandably gave rise to a trend that saw many ladies tending to nurture dreams of becoming betrothed, prodded by desire for financial security, to sailors. This was true to such extent that when suitors of a lady included a professional and a sailor, the woman often chose the sailor. It was then that a popular joke on this was born and retold at public social functions: "Whenever a mother of a courted lady receives at home a visit by her daughter's suitor who is a professional, she would express her gladness by saying, 'Ay, salamat, napa-dalaw kayo!' or, in English, 'Oh, thanks; you've visited!' But if the visiting suitor happens to be a USN sailor, the mother would even more gladly say, 'Ay, salamat, napa-dollar kayo!' or, in English, 'Oh, thanks; you're a dollar!'"

Although intended purely for humor, this joke nevertheless appears to most Subic folks realistically reflective of what simply is truth. Many former young ladies of Subic are today in the U.S. only because of their having become brides of USN sailors who got stationed in Subic, or inducted into the U.S. Navy via the Subic Bay Naval Base. But second thoughts tend to suggest that perhaps love, coupled with desire for financial security, is what ultimately counts as the strongest motivating factor behind a Subiquenian Juliet's particular eye for and betrothal to a USN Romeo. Subiquenian ladies, both professionals and otherwise, known to have married USN servicemen, are shown in Appendix C—in the order of their family or matrimonial names, as the case may be.

"Social Box" Fad

A relevant occurrence of some significance from the period was that of USN Filipino sailors' going around town in a car or lording it over others with a "social box," a feature of a gala dance or a fiesta-tinged ballroom event. Sights like this greatly enhanced sailor swains' enjoyment of finding themselves often a particular cynosure of lasses' attention.

Purposely intended for a festivity's fund-raising, a "social box" is a prize—usually a gift-wrapped fried chicken or roasted pork—awarded to a bidder who has paid, usually in a crowded, glittering auditorium, the largest amount of cash for a special solo dance with a pre-designated lady dance partner. Most often, Filipino sailors emerged winning bidders, with themselves being catapulted in the process into an evening's ephemeral but nonetheless avidly vied-for limelight. Social occasions enlivened this way, which usually were well attended by the young, often proved greatly instrumental in enabling sailor guys to enjoy surer chances of winning the hearts of prospected Subiquenian gals.

Civic Spirit in Action

In matters of civic work requiring purely volunteered time and effort, Subic-based USN sailors, regardless of ethnicity, demonstrated an inveterate propensity for not being behind as well. To help promote close and friendly relations, groups of them periodically participated in community outreach projects like repairing or repainting schools—not only in Subic but also in neighboring towns. In emergencies resulting from typhoons and other disastrous calamities, U.S. Marine first-aid-rescue teams always volunteered, dispensing multiple kinds of help—food, medical care, equipment, etc.—where it was greatly needed.

A Popular Hollywood Movie Shooting in Subic

Because of the good rapport between Subic citizens and the Subic Bay U.S. Naval Base's population, not to mention a certainty of ready help in exigencies, it was in Subic that Hollywood located the filming of *An American Guerrilla in the Philippines*. Filmed in 1949, the World War II-themed movie starred Tyrone Power and employed some Subic folks as extras. Some of them were recruited with the help of Eliseo Labampa, a senior and president of the student body organization of the Subic Educational Institute, which is now known as the Saint James High School. He and many others who participated, retains up to this day a vivid memory of the film's scene showing Subic's Ilwas Catholic Cemetery where Tyrone Power paid moral tribute to a fallen pal who was interred thereat. Even in a remote sense, the selection of Subic for that movie-making event obviously had something to do with Subic Bay's budding fame as one of the world's distinctively interesting travel spots.

Subic Bay's Bonus Economic Worth

As indeed nature's prestige-creative life giver, Subic Bay sees itself also serving—and wisely harnessed—in a way that is purely industry-oriented. In Subic's Asinan Proper began being erected in 1979 a sea-based industrial complex—the Subic Shipyard and Engineering Inc. (formerly PHILSECO), a harbor facility catering solely to multinational ships' repair and other servicing routines. Now the biggest shipyard in the Philippines, it generates annual revenues that sustain substantial cash outlays for Subic's municipal expense budget. Its economy-pillaring role for Subic is expected to be expand in the near future because of its upcoming promise of 20, 000 jobs projected to be generated by the HANJIN Heavy Industrial Corporation, a South Korean shipbuilding company.

When the U.S. Navy was in Subic, its economy was fundamentally dollar-powered. Even though the combined industrial operations of PHILSECO and HANJIN demonstrate further progress, they don't get make up for the loss of the revenue brought in by the U.S. Navy.

This is understandable. In addition to the dollar flow from the economy-buttressing home budgets of U.S. citizens domiciled in the Subic-Olongapo area, and money spent by sailors disgorged by periodically visiting USN ships, workers' pay rates in their naval base jobs were relatively higher, compared to present-day standards. This higher pay rate was what made it possible, in most cases, for many of the Subiquenian professionals—doctors, nurses, med-techs, teachers, engineers, etc.—now enjoying life in the U.S. or anywhere else throughout the world, to afford the financial demands of college education during their student days. Their parents' income simply got greatly bolstered by the progressive businesses they engaged in or whatever U.S. Navy civilian jobs they had held.

MUNICIPALITY'S POPULATION

As is true of most other progressive Philippine towns, Subic is populated with people representing various ethnicities known by the dialects they use. In Appendix D can be seen Subic's eleven ethnically heterogeneous groups constituting its overall population. The largest group is Tagalog; it comprises 82.88% of total. Ilocano is next, but only has 5.37%. Largely in a descending order, the rest are Cebuano, 2.36%; Zambal, 2.36%; Kampampangan, 1.82%; Waray, 1.28%- Samal, 0.88%; Bicol, 0.62%; Ilongo, 0.46%

Masbateno-, 0.38%; and unknown/combined others, including Muslims, 1.59%.

The existence of this multiple ethnicity is ascribed mainly to the decades-long stay of the U.S. Navy in Subic. It attracted through the years the influx of people who were impelled to migrate from other places throughout the Philippines, understandably out of quest for job and/or business opportunities.

The Philippines geographically exists as a non-contiguous land of some 7,000 islands separated by distances of less than or more than a mile from one another. This to some extent explains the dialectal diversity of its people—a sociological fact born out of its being sprawled apart with a variety of ethnicity-based cultures characteristic of it as a whole. This situation may appear reflected in Subic, but it is with respect, at the most, to the diverseness of the town's population groups only—not necessarily to culture, traditions, etc.

In a population survey conducted in 2005 by the Subic Health Center under the direction of its head, Dr. Leonardo Afable, Jr., and based on records under the care of Gloria A. Cruz and Loreta L. Lapazon, health clinic staff members, it was estimated that 80,105 people currently live in Subic. In 2001, its total population was 63,019 (from 13,882 households) as compared to only 57,099 in 1995 (from 12,040 households). This shows that from 2001 to 2005, Subic's population increased by 17,086 or 21% and from 1995 to 2001, by 5,920 or 10%. Population distribution, in the descending order by barangay in 2001, was as follows: Calapacuan, 10,925; Cawag, 7,181; Matain, 6,758; Calapandayan, 6,080; Mangan-vaca, 4,691; Santo Tomas, 3,974; San Isidro, 3,890; Asinan Proper, 3,684; Aningway-Sacatihan, 3,185- Ilwas, 3,017; Baraca-Camachile, 2,828; Pamatawan, 2,514, Wawandue, 1,542- Naugsol, 1,360; Batiawan, 787; and Asinan Poblacion, 603.

Of Subic's entire population in 1995, about 72% was estimated by the Philippine National Statistics Office to be living in urban areas and the rest or 28%, in rural areas.

The most urbanized Subic poblacion, which daily teems with busy, on-the-move people—it being the center of business, governmental affairs, etc., appears the most densely populated. It has the highest number of people per unit of land area. What is known to be once a "neglected wetland" that reverted to being part of public domain a hundred meters or so to the east of the Subic Municipal Hall, whose site was that of a past Subic Public Market called Baraca, had become inhabitable via manual reclamation, and the whole area is now studded with permanent homes.

Traffic Inconvenience as a Result of Population Increase

The rise in Subic's population over the years now sees a rise, too, in the need for normalizing traffic in its thoroughfares. Up to the 1990s, traffic in its streets was not a much of a problem. People could travel to anywhere in the town conveniently by any means of transportation. And if travel was to be made by foot, one could feel quite at ease in doing so, because there was plenty of room to move around; in other words, there was not much to worry about dangers usually associated with traffic-congested streets. But today, various motor vehicles—buses, jeeps, cars, and tricycles—fill Subic's main roads.

And in barrios, "pedicabs" (bicycles with side cabs) abound for travelers who prefer going to-and-from their homes and in mainstream traffic without walking. This scenario goes on almost throughout all hours of each day, particularly in the poblacion, so that hand-signaled traffic control by members of Traffic Management Brigade (TMB) has become a necessity in busy crossings to help forestall accidents and ensure travel safety.

Components of Population Citizenship

By citizenship, the great majority of Subic's populace is composed of Filipinos. Other nationals include Australians and Koreans, but the most numerous are Americans—about 0.18% of the total population.

CULTURE

Religion

Subic's citizens are predominantly Roman Catholics and the rest are Aglipayans, Iglesia ni Cristo (INC), and Born Again Christians. Muslims reached the town in the early 1960s with the establishment of a Muslim fishing community in Barangay Matain, where there are now about three hundred (300) families belonging to the faith.

In the practice of their own Christian faith, most of Subic's Roman Catholics do so most commonly by hearing Holy Mass on Sundays. They also attend special masses such as those held during the Christmas season and the Holy Week. In addition, where their time allows, they get themselves involved in one or more of church organizations, of which the Holy Name

Society, St. James Parish Pastoral Council, Legion of Mary, Knights of Columbus, Couples for Christ, Collectors Guild, Lectors and Commentators Group, and Apostleship of Prayer are the most well known.

Among the relatively more religious, the making of a panata or solemn promise for certain purposes is also a common practice. Such purposes are usually personal in nature—to atone for a committed sin, to show gratitude for a fulfilled want, or to undergo self-sacrifice for realizing a certain yearning. Doing so usually takes the form of one's indulgence in self-infliction of pain or penitence done on Lent, in Novena prayers, or in knee walking inside a church while praying.

Flagellation as a Particular Act of Faith

Flagellation is a faith manifestation, a kind of penitence. Its adherents—normally men only—keep their identities unknown by having their heads hooded with black pieces of cloth while in the act of beating themselves repeatedly—on minutely blood-oozing skin wounds on their backs as they walk in the street. They beat themselves with a kind of whip made of a rope as handle and of several bamboo sticks of five-six inches each as impact pieces. Prior to their penitential street march, their back skin wounds are prepared among themselves in a secretly pre-chosen group rendezvous, using the sharpest of broken bottle pieces. Where there are kubols or makeshift sheds built for the holding of Passion Plays as a separate form of Holy Week observance, the flagellants would kneel and pray in front, alone or in groups. Their march in the street begins on Holy Thursday and culminates on Holy Friday—with an abrupt bath in a river somewhere.

The fact that practitioners do not get sick at all against their prolonged exposure to the sun, the repeated beatings of their back wounds under an unclean condition, and their outright plunge into a river that invites risky sudden temperature change is seen to only heighten their faith in God.

Customary Gestures of Respect

In Subic, the age-old custom of children showing respect for their parents still exists. On visits or on once-in-a-while chance meetings anywhere, the child takes a hand—extended or not—of a parent/godparent or an older relative, puts it on his or her forehead, and says, "Mano po!" As a side purpose, the gesture automatically means a receiving—in the child's favor—of the moral blessings of the person paid obeisance to.

Filipinos have earned a positive reputation for this, as people from other parts of the world recognizing that it is conducive to family solidarity. It's has such significance that a Filipino movie was made with the title, *Mano po!* and it has become, in recent months, one of a widely advertised film spectacle that stayed for some time in media.

Symbolism of the Filipino Word "Po"

In any interaction that involves oral or written communication, Subic's adolescents are wont to add the one-syllable word, "po," at any appropriate part of what they say to adults. To them, its use signifies the highest degree of showing respect as a fundamental requisite of human nicety for social contacts or relationships of non-family or of just a casual nature. If the word, "ho," is used instead, it likewise bespeaks of a show of respect, but it is uttered usually when an addressee is an equal in age. Non-usage of either is seen as normal among family members, relatives, or friends who are generally young or adults, but it is used among strangers of a more-or-less similar maturity level.

On the other hand, if neither po nor ho is used by adolescents in talking with adults, it is usually construed as self-revelatory of one's home breeding in matters of personal manners—if not of arrogance. In Subic, it is common knowledge that very seldom, if ever, do people go about in their dealings with others arrogantly. Psychologists' explain that arrogance or any other negative behavior is nothing more than a self-deluding, compensatory mechanism for what is but usually a mediocre, if not totally impoverished character clothed with a "high-hat" sense of self-importance or over-bearing pride.

Indigenous Conversational Expression

In all of Zambales or anywhere in the Philippines, it is only in Subic where indigenous folks are habituated with always saying or adding the expression, "ay" in their conversations with others. This one-syllable word is often used at the beginning or the end of every statement they make in conversing with people, and these are two examples of how it is said: "Ay, dumating na sila!" and "Hindi ko naman sila nakita, ay." In English, these mean, respectively: "Oh, they have arrived already!" and "I did not see them." It is thus that if one hears any stranger talking in Tagalog who repeatedly uses ay in making statements, there is always a great certainty that the stranger hails from Subic. It simply has become a distinguishing mark for native Subicquenians—hence, the birth of the "Subic Ay Festival" as enacted by Municipal Regulatory Ordinance No. 2002-04 through Municipal Resolution No. 52. How "ay" originated or developed as a part of Subic's culture is unknown.

Town Fiesta: A Foremost Social Tradition

As in most other Philippine towns, social gatherings, such as weddings, baptisms, birthday parties, post-burials, Ascension Day (called ika-apatnapong araw), and other occasions held for celebrating events are customarily religion-tinged practices with multi-course meals. These form an important part of the culture of Subic folks. But as a purely family affair, any celebration falling within the category of any one of these occasions is often seen as somehow a measure of the hosting family's socio-economic status. Any socially festive event that sees a generally community-wide involvement, where every individual or family, regardless of status, has every opportunity to uninhibitedly participate in or enjoy all that goes with it, that occasion is called the Subic Town Fiesta.

Religion as Precursor of Subic's Town Fiesta

In essence, religion is involved in the holding of Subic's town fiesta; it is the source of its beginnings. Its celebration is fundamentally for commemorating Subic's supposed gratitude to its Patron Saint James or Mahal na Poong San Tiago (in Tagalog). A purely legendary story from the Spanish regime in the Philippines tells that the notorious Chinese pirate Limahong had once made Subic a particular quarry for his predatory raids. But by what seemed to be a miracle, one of the revoltos, or human images inside the Subic Catholic Church that was mounted on a graven image of a horse, just suddenly rushed one night to a nearby shore where Limahong was disembarking with his cohorts from his pirate ship. The never-before-seen figure, atop a horse galloping back and forth on the shore as if leading an armed force poised for a defensive attack from the dark, instilled such fear in Limahong that he, right there and then, retreated to his ship with his fellow pirates—and vowed never to set foot in Subic again. The figure—as the legend said—was the image of Saint James mounted on a horse, and it was then that Subic had made him its patron saint, with a commemorative procession held every year in his honor, from that time on, as a gesture of gratitude. The annual event is called, "Feast of Saint James."

Fiesta's Purely Social Aspect

On the other hand, the holding of a fiesta in Subic is also seen as an occasion for a town-wide merry-making enlivened with marching bands, multi-themed parade, public dancing, family hospitality sharing via home-tendered feasts, and a miscellany of other socially-oriented, to-see-and-be-seen-based cultural activities.

The celebration's first day, called disperas, is ushered in by the arrival of marching bands that go through main thoroughfares. On the following evening, a coronation ball is held. For open-air viewing by as much audience as could be accommodated inside and outside, Subic's Town Plaza-Auditorium outdoor facility is often used as venue. The highlight of the popular, profusely crowded affair consists of the presentation and crowning of the fiesta queen and her three damas or princesses. In a cultural sense, the queen represents the Philippines as a motherland country, and the three princesses, Luzon, Mindanao, and Visayas—its three main islands.

Usually, a musical-literary program centering on formal tributes to the occasion's four ball-gowned lady cynosures as they are seated—with their respective, formally attired bachelor escorts standing by their side—precedes the symbolical crowning ceremony.

Complemented with a stereo sound system and with a hired orchestra for the inherent joys of live music, the program is interspersed with song, poem, and folk dance presentations rendered by special participants. As the attention-drawing ceremony goes on, synchronized rocket fireworks shoot up brightly and then explode loudly into the air—as a momentary sky spectacle to enhance the symbolic significance of what is being beheld amid the night's gathering. A dance for all is an additional highlight for everyone's enjoyment of the rest of the evening—and it usually lasts until the wee hours of the ensuing morning.

Depending on finances, the fiesta's second day is highlighted mainly with the holding of a sports competition, a talent contest, and a cultural parade of multi-themed floats and of diversely participating public and private organizations and their members, and marching bands of two or more origins. The sports competition, often held in the town plaza, mainly for the benefit of young contestants, usually includes such outdoor games as sack races, slippery bamboo climbing, blindfolded pot hitting, and basketball. For the talent contest, which is always open to everyone, amateur singing is what eager participants mainly vie for amidst a throng of both the young and the old. Winners in the contest—like in the sports competition—are customarily awarded with cash or material prizes.

In the cultural parade, the main float carries the fiesta queen and her three damas, along with their respective escorts. This float and the others are fittingly decorated with multiple paint colors, ribbons, flowers, and leaves, as are the others that go with it. The parade is usually watched by people of all walks of life as it passes by in Subic's main streets, for which onlookers often would begin lining up once the sounds of the bands accompanying it fill the air. When it ends, after lunch, the parade bands later regroup in the town plaza for a concert exhibition, to the delight and entertainment of the general public.

Showering of Fiesta Hospitality

For visiting friends and relatives, invited or not, before or on the day of the fiesta families are wont to provide hospitality by way of a home banquet with multi-courses and lechon plus assorted drinks. As an inherent aspect of human nature, the social and economic standing of any Subic family often gets associated by people with the number of fiesta guests that are entertained by a family's richly betokened hospitality. It is thus that there always had been families in Subic known to be not given to being hesitant if asked by fiesta organizers to serve as volunteer hosts—normally on a one-group-one-banquet-per-family basis—to even a sizable group of band members hired for the fiesta.

Fiesta guests are usually accorded as well invitations to its queen's ball— a dancing event with the event's queen, princesses, and all their escorts present. Usually, it is participated in mostly by the young at heart. But for balance, a free option is always left open to those whose age or personal taste lacks a liking or knack for dancing: a pre-contracted zarzuela or musical-drama-comedy show is simultaneously presented in a separate, also open-air venue. The repertoire of general family fun and entertainment of the zarzuela group usually results in a show that is usually as thickly crowded as the fiesta's coronation night.

Mang Magpoc Becomes Popular with Fiesta Queen Floats

Because of his artful craftsmanship, a man known to have emigrated from Bataan to Subic became one of the town's most successful painters. Shortly after establishing residence for his family at Wawandue, one of four main barrios constituting the Subic poblacion, Mang Magpoc, a name for which he became popularly known to most Subicquenians, had the good fortune of having become the favorite painter of the incumbent Municipal, Mayor Dangal Guevara. Mang Magpoc's art works ranged from business signboard letterings to designs and drawings attractively emphasizing the significance of certain social or historical events during the holding of traditional public functions like Independence Day celebrations.

It was thus that—mainly by the strength of his painting talent alone—not to mention his good practice of human relations, Mang Magpoc was perennially hired by Mayor Guevara for taking charge of all painting and decorative works in the preparation of fiesta floats, particularly the float for the event's ceremonial queen and princesses, on the holding of Subic's Annual Town Fiesta. Mang Magpoc is now deceased, but his children are known to be now all in the U.S., and the oldest is Phillip C. Magpoc, a retired USN sailor who presently serves as one of the members of the board of directors of the Subic Association of San Diego.

Fiesta's Particular Appeal Among Subiquenian Lasses

All because of the seemingly irresistible lure of being a fiesta's particular focus for the general public's adulation amid the glitter and fanfare spiriting it, to be a fiesta queen has a strong appeal among Subic's lasses—and chances of being just a runner-up to it for a consolation outcome are also valued. Regardless of its promised cash award, the greatest single motivating factor behind its appeal stems from the great mass of Subic's citizenry's equation of the opportunity of being proclaimed so with a social episode of once-in-a-lifetime fame and honor.

The enjoyable experience from the festivity is only ephemeral—all of the moments of fame accorded its mass-adulated honorees are bound to disappear as soon as it ends, but this is seen somehow compensated for. In addition to video and camera photography, usually pre-readied to record in print the festivity's noteworthy activities, copies of a pre-printed souvenir program containing pictures of the fiesta queen and her damas with their respective escorts and those of fiesta officials and other VIP's are handed out—as a particularly valued lifetime memento.

Understandably intended for posterity's knowledge and remembrance, the cherished keepsake is usually in the form of a photo-filled packet of information collected, designed, and presented in the nature of a who's who fashion show, naming fiesta honorees, committees, well-wishing fund donors, patrons, business establishments, etc. Production costs for it are often far exceeded by the revenues it reaps in the form of fees paid for business advertisements in its pages, not to mention payments (deemed donations) by individuals or families for pre-priced spaces for their own photos and complimentary wishes and greetings in its other pages. Among most Subic homes, the material is usually kept the way family photo albums are, and casually used for entertaining visitors during home social gatherings.

Determining Winners of Fiesta Beauty Contest

To be considered for a Subic fiesta queen candidacy normally requires a pre-set measure of standards-based popularity anchored on physical, moral, or intellectual attributes or talents contestants are expected to possess. As main criteria, these factors are not overlooked in selecting candidates, but actual practice often ends up favoring a different criteria. In most cases, money is what always ultimately determines actual winners. The reason for this is that whoever of up to 16 candidates gets individually selected from Subic's 16 barangays, only the top four who turn in the highest cash proceeds from the sale of ballots issued to them for raising fiesta funds would end up as winners. And whoever of the four of them emerges the highest ballot seller is automatically adjudged queen.

Thus, for amor propio or self-esteem, it has become anything but rare that a prestige-motivated clan would spend their own or borrowed money, just to ensure a doted daughter's becoming a Subic fiesta queen. To be so simply is to most people an enviable winning of the social limelight of instant popularity and prestige built on a foundation of financial strength, be this achieved purely via sold ballots or not—bona fide public endorsement set aside.

Cultural Evolution

As a material incentive, all the four highest fiesta ballot sellers get a pre-set percentage from the gross cash proceeds of their ballot disposal. But if the ball gowns or terno, and other personal things a winner needs to buy and wear for each night and day of the fiesta's two-day duration actually costs more than estimates, end result is inevitably at her own expense. While this sounds inhibiting of one's interest to be a fiesta queen candidate, there is no shortage of contestants for it among fiesta enthusiasts or organizers.

But because of problems arising from a plethora of causes, like financial/internal control loopholes (including pecuniary mal-interest), time-effaced values, commodity cost increases, people's upgraded expectations, etc., the holding of a fiesta in Subic has become irregular over the years. Since the 1980s, its celebration started being done on an only-as-needed basis. This trend applies as well—but for different reasons open only to conjecture—to what used to be Subic's other almost-annually-held social-oriented traditions. One of them is Santa Cruz de Mayo, an event characterized with a procession of culturally symbolic princes and princesses and a pabitin (a hanging trellis with candies tied to it for kids). Another is San Juan or Feast of Saint John, an event celebrated with a surprise splashing of water at street passers-by, regardless of whether they are friends or total strangers. Still another is the serenading of a lady below her window at night by those paying court to her. The songs sung would be love songs (or **kundimans**) with the accompaniment of a guitar. And then there is the All Saints' Day house-to-house serenade, a nocturnal group activity undertaken for receiving voluntary cash handouts (by families serenaded). These age-old traditions are no longer as popular as they were decades ago.

But since the onset of the present municipal administration, the Subic town fiesta started being observed with some innovations instead of fading into oblivion—as is the case with the town's other social traditions. Money solicitation via sale of fiesta beauty contest ballots, souvenir program pre-paid business ads and pre-priced personal/family greetings, "social box," and benefit dances are no longer practiced. In place of socially entertaining the general public with programs featuring a symbolical queen and princesses, the municipal fiesta committee arranges with all community sectors involved—church, school, civic group, etc.—for their respective participating contributions, and this is ordinarily by way of appropriate cultural activities predominated by prize-awarded contests in folk dancing, athletic games, banca racing, singing, instrumental music, etc. "And instead of fiesta expenses being shouldered by the general public," describes Barangay Kagawad Danny Caramol of Baraca-Camachile, "budget funding is statutorily pre-allocated by the municipal government out of barrio income."

Calapandayan's Barrio Fiesta

Towards the north, Calapandayan geographically sets as the first barrio closely adjacent to the Subic poblacion. Demarcating its boundary with the town proper is a bridge, which used to be a platform for hurling down dynamite for occasional fishing, as well as being a platform for public diving by swimming enthusiasts. It is the only Subic barrio that annually holds a fiesta on a scale approximating that of Subic itself as a whole. There are two reasons. First is that Calapandayan has its own patron saint, San Roque, whose image is mounted aboard a banca for leading an annual daytime procession of barrio folks riding also in bancas in the Calapandayan sea, with the event being called "karakul." Secondly, the main entertainment for the general public is the presentation of what has customarily become interchangeably known as the "comedia" or "moro-moro."

As a culture uniquely restricted only to Calapandayan in all Subic barangays, it is staged as a traditional spectacle preeminently conducted with choreographed, artful sword fighting-dancing movements with simultaneous poetical readings enunciated in Ilocano. Calapandayan's inhabitants are mostly Ilocanos, known to have originated from Zambales's Ilocano-speaking towns: San Marcelino, San Antonio, San Narciso, and San Felipe, on the main.

The event's partakers wear multi-colored, from-shoulder-to-ankle costumes fashioned generally in the manner of silken clothing worn by Chinese laymen and royalty of olden times. It ebbed in popularity, however, not long after the war, with aging, if not life transition, among the culture's usual practitioners and supporters being the chief cause.

Other Barrios' Fiestas

Other Subic barrios also annually hold smaller fiestas of their own. Religious fervor inspires processions of homage for an adopted saint. Where there is Ilwas' barrio fiesta called Santacruzan in honor of Mahal na Krus, fiestas in other barrios are celebrated in honor also of their own patron/patroness. Typically, Calapacuan's fiesta is in honor of Our Lady of Pillar; Matain's, Saint Anthony de Padua; Sto.Tomas', St. Thomas; San Isidro's, St. Isidore; Naugsol's, St. Peter the Rock; and Manggahan's, Santo Nino.

Cockfighting as a Social Tradition

In Subic, cockfighting is seen as a seemingly timeless tradition that is essentially social in nature. It dovetails with one's gregariousness for keeping up inter-personal relationships in a gathering enlivened with know-and-be-known-tinged motivations. In addition, money, chance, and skill motivate participants. "Gambling!" is what one would most likely call this, but it simply is the only kind of a matter of factly social occasion participated in by throngs of the relatively more mature for all the excitement and fun they as enthusiasts find in and associate with it. As a socially-oriented pastime engaged in on weekends town-wide by people of all walks of life, by rich and poor alike, cockfighting is actually a legalized-gambling sport in the Philippines. People love it for its non-plastic opportunities for personal popularity build-up and casual manifestation of socio-economic status or of fulfillment of words of honor.

Ordinarily held in a privately owned cockfight stadium, its afficionados or waging participants offer bets with or without gamecocks of their own. Like other forms of sports, the game requires pertinently developed skills. This applies not only to the game cocks pitted against each other (normally only two for every contest) but also to their handlers, as well as to the parties responsible for attaching each bird's razor-sharp steel spur that it is to use in its fight with its opponent.

Cockfighting bets run to as high or as low as amounts wagers for each contest are prepared to offer or accept. Experienced plain wagers, bet callers, or cock handler-wagers are known to invariably share the advice that employing utmost common sense and alertness, rather than just relying on luck, is a key to ensuring greater chances for winning bets.

The sport has become a durably favorite pastime not only in Subic but practically anywhere throughout the Philippines. As most kinds of national sports in other countries with respect to its crowd-attracting appeal, it is accessible to people of all walks of life: to professionals or laymen. Seen as an easy, open means of earning money, especially among knowledgeable enthusiasts, it has no limits on low bets, so even a less-moneyed wager is totally free to participate in waging for any contest. Also, a bet could win substantially by more than its equivalent at a pre-agreed condition that necessitates no written contract or use of any kind of chips or tokens. Any bet, routinely just voiced out or signaled by fingers, is a word of honor by which everyone is customarily bound to abide in exercise of personal integrity, on pain of—although quite a rarity—severe retribution, including game debarment in case of a violation. Another reason for the game's popularity stems from every contest's characteristic excitements as it ends within only a couple of minutes or so, with—amidst a crowd's instinctively yelled-out calls and cheers—a win's sure returns being paid instantly.

Cockfighting Game's Effect on Human Relations

The fact that indulgence in the game effectively bridges gaps between or among neighbors into strong bonds of personal alliances and camaraderie is well known. Subic neighbors raising fighting cocks often find themselves on certain mornings voluntarily huddled together with their respective game birds held by their tail feathers in their midst. Their purpose is simply to hone their respective gamecocks' fighting prowess and skill.

The sharing this way of their common interests—at times up to a point of deciding on combining resources for a pre-set visit to a cockfight arena with a pooled sum of bets—is a predisposition to friendship that usually lasts for as long as they are on the sports.

But to others, cockfighting is seen unfavorably. Some people see it as a game that smacks of animal cruelty. Others look at it as an unconstructive use of time.

And then there are those who see its perilous nature, it being a knife-equipped kind of sports hand-staged amid a crowd-filled arena for the spectacle of two fighting cocks' instinct-driven, fight-to-death duel—seemingly the very source of excitement that enthusiasts feel about it, along with bet results prospected. Although known to be quite rare, there actually was once an instance where a fighting cock's handler was wounded almost fatally as the game bird he was holding just suddenly went wild and attacked him instead of its supposed opponent. The victim's bracing of his arms to parry off the razor-sharp-spurred leg blows thrown by the attacking bird was to no avail, and this was headlined in newspapers.

Aside from this particular negative aspect of the sports, there also had been actual instances where—although also a rarity—unscrupulousness of certain wagers reneging on placed bets had inevitably resulted in serious disputes. A typical case of fatal consequence actually occurred in Subic when, apparently because of abuse of position. A certain barrio official, for having repeatedly reneged on his lost cockfight wagers, just suddenly fell down to an unknown assailant's bullet in a cockfight arena.

Another known negativity of the game is its adverse effects on conjugal living. In Subic, the number of occurrences of marital spats that often originate from husbands' substantial cockfighting losses are not unknown. Among Subic friends is an oft-told joke, with husbands as the butt: "Your wife will again shove you off your bed's mosquito net if your bets see you back home with empty pocket!"

Family Values as Mirrored in Land Ownership

Owning any kind of a piece of land is ordinarily considered one indicator of a family's socio-economic status in Subic. For this reason, its has become more or less an integral part of the culture of Subic folks to ensure that the land they are living on or occupying for farming or for any other purpose is covered or registered with a duly recognized or legitimate ownership documents. But most families only possess tax declarations on the lands they live on as residential lots or own as homesteads, and only a few actually possess titles to whatever land property they own.

Regardless of several identifiable factors that could actually account for this, "land grabbing" thus became over the years a grievous problem that rendered no few landholders in the town innocent victims. It occurred even during the martial-law years, and up to this day cases centering on land ownership disputes filed in court take a long time to get resolved.

Actually, it is human nature's dark side—or simply greed—that accounts for what could only be construed as the devilish aspect of land grabbing in Subic—an anomalous way of titling lands that are either already titled legitimately or just covered with tax declarations by existing owners holding just deeds of sale. Thus, it is only the ultimate arbiter of legal conflicts—the Supreme Court—that is relied upon by the general public for the final solution of its lay constituents' land ownership problems as created by the unscrupulous elements of society.

Community Organizations

Many Subicquenians, particularly young adults, are fond of being identified with certain organizations for reasons as divergent in nature as such organizations' purposes, and socialization in spheres of more-or-less similar age if not reputation levels. In the late 1950s, right in the Subic poblacion was organized the Subic Market Citizens' Club, with Subic

Municipal Treasurer Maximo Pante as beginning president. Acronymed and called Submarcit Club, it was formed not necessarily for any purpose having to do with organizers' or prospected members' being engaged or involved in affairs of a market but simply because its jurisdictional service area, the poblacion itself, happened to be then still customarily called "Baraca"—the English equivalent of which is "market."

As was true of most other neighborhood organizations anywhere else at the time, its activities were fundamentally social—dancing, partying, etc. It lasted only for less than a decade, but the memory it left later ushered in the mushrooming of other organizations of various names and denominations in Subic. In the 1960s, barrio associations started to rise in each of Subic's 16 barangays. Then between the 1970s and the mid-1980s, the Balikatan sa Kaunlaran associational fad practically duplicated what the Subic Annual Town Fiesta used to be held for. It raised funds for civic community improvement projects via popularity contests, organized multi-sector parades, and held ballroom dancing. And it even came forth with an innovation: It included even married couples—particularly from among those engaged in business—as candidates for the popularity jousts conducted throughout its heyday years. Even if matters of management and utilization of (socially) raised funds elicited much criticisms form the general public, not much could be done about it mainly by virtue of political inter-relations under the situation.

And from the 1980s to the late 2000s, three relatively more distinctive, prestigious organizational groups—the Lions, Rotary Club, and Jaycees, all known to be of an even international stature, virtually vied with one another in dominating Subic's social scenario. Each carried on a miscellany of civic/volunteer work benefiting the general public as a whole and the less fortunate in particular. They donated public thoroughfare fixtures—waiting sheds, road signs, etc., and conducted special free medical-dental services for the needy, as well. Being affiliated with any one of them was known to entail a heavier toll on one's wallet, but the still-ongoing operations of the Subic Bay U.S. Naval Base at the time, in its incidental role as practically a pillar to many Subic families' budget, was simply an auspiciously respondent blessing.

Organizations Among Subiquenian Expatriates

Certain differences expatriates see in their chosen new homeland serve as a predisposing factor for prodding them to identify or go along with their kind as peers of common origin. As an affirmative reflection of the truth of the common adage, "Birds of the same feather stay together," this is well exemplified by and among expatriates in the U.S. who originated from Subic. In California particularly, former Subic citizens who had become naturalized, and even those awaiting naturalization had become connected, in varying capacities and duration, with organizations generally simulating, in nature or purpose, a voluntary neighborhood association. Understandably, the strongest single motivation behind any typical organization's existence is seen to reside with the social aspects of the activities it occasionally undertakes under whatever resources it could come up with—in both human and material form.

Up to five associations of past Subic citizens, exclusive of those from Olongapo, are known to be in existence today in the U.S. As is the case with some other associations that are named mostly after their respective towns of origin in the Philippines, though, problems mainly of loose responsibility and accountability, undue authority, transparency, and self-serving rather than member-oriented ends have remained a bane to the operations and progress of each. Because of this, what is left of the entire associational scene is just a few officers persistently dealing with not-easy-to-maintain participation of supposedly active members, whose knack for social occasions like reunion-/fiesta-oriented dinner-dance, outdoor partying, etc. is simply not reliable enough for maintaining associational solidarity.

Common Expatriates' Associational Problem

Lack of "active membership"—i.e., supposed members' maintained participation in the fundamental routines of organizational affiliation, foremost of which is regular payment of membership fees—is the most significant indication of recalcitrance among prospected association members. This problem is attributable to several causes—like lack of time, far residence, personal differences, etc.—but the most directly relevant with is certainly the way associational affairs are run. In this regard, these actual instances are typical. Where and when association officers were once supposed to be elected via standard procedures, i.e., with prior formal nominations, their election was done brazenly, without prior notice to the candidates themselves, save for those predetermined as (already) winners. In other words, the election was railroaded, with the names of pre-chosen candidates of greater popularity arbitrarily just pitted against those of less popularity, by way of a list mailed as ballots. It all smacked of a seemingly smart but ultimately self-destructive design of tricky manipulation, rendering electoral outcome garnered on the basis more of popularity, rather than ability or familiarity. The consequence was disunity.

On another instance, where an associational financial report was supposed to reflect either "surplus" or "deficit" in a procedural expenditure-versus-revenue reckoning, the ending balance was made to appear exactly "0" (zero), thereby inevitably creating the impression that pertinent figures were made to reflect not reality but falsity—in short, they were doctored!

Then, there was that time in 1989 when a Subic-style fiesta queen contest was held in California under the auspices of two or more associations—with the winning queen contestant's emergence as such being brazenly made to materialize only because of "borrowed association funds." For the purpose of ensuring a relative's victory in the contest, the spouse of a key officer of the association represented by a contestant used her influence in having association funds appropriated as sort of a (personal) loan needed to make her relative emerge fiesta queen. The coronation night was held in Southern California, and it was crowded—with even the presence of the incumbent Subic mayor of the time—who had made an abrupt overseas flight. But that event started and ushered in the downfall of the association—in terms of active membership and/or normal functioning—that was represented by the winner-queen.

And lastly, when once a well-meaning packet of proposals with illustrated far-reaching effects projected as multifariously and mutually beneficial to all concerned were once presented for scrutiny and subsequent possible adoption, "That's a scam!" was what a purported association director remarked of it—ostensibly in a tone self-signifying anything but knowledge adequacy.

In light of these problems, which typically characterize some, if not all, of Subic associations in the U.S., if not anywhere else, members have become skeptical about participating, with the associations perpetually bogging down in dysfunction, as a result. Some have observed that the organizations are existent in name only, if not for ego or show only, and their active officers always outnumber their active members (in spirit or supposed obligations).

The Olongapo-Subic Bay Association's Aid to Aetas

Although an association not purely of Subiquenians but composed of past residents of Olongapo, Cavite, and Subic itself, the Olongapo-Subic Bay Association (acronym-ed OSBA) once became particularly appreciable in Northern California, as well as in Olongapo City. Its president was then Manny Bernal, a civil engineer who had worked in the Subic Bay U.S. Naval Base but now was a long-time resident of Union City, California.

During his administration of OSBA in the 1990s, it substantially aided in kind all of the minority Aetas serving as volunteers helping safeguard—from human environmental predators—the still almost virginal forests that shifted into the care of the Subic Bay Metropolitan Authority (SBMA) when the U.S. Navy pulled out of Subic at the time. Heavy-duty ponchos were donated to the Aetas, and the first SBMA chairman, Mayor Richard J. Gordon, appreciated the association's concerns. Its humanitarian help saw print in California's Philippine News, and a write-up was read in a program in which outstanding donors and supporters were awarded special certificates of appreciation.

But in subsequent years OSBA had changed its name, and it known as the "Ulo ng Apo Association in America." The reason for the change is known only to whoever initiated it. As it was, when OSBA's presidency transferred to others, copies of an Olongapo City political candidate's letter addressed to the association for campaign fund solicitation were circulated among prospected supporters—but in vain: no one positively responded. The candidate was on the other side of the fence, facing a Gordon-named opponent.

Regard for Education

Among most Subic families, education is a paramount priority—next to life and health—in parental concerns for affairs of the home. Deemed a form of wealth its possessor could lastingly enjoy and carry intact anywhere, it is viewed particularly by the poor as the only path to freedom from the shackles of a daily living of hand-to-mouth existence. It is thus that, as is true of most Filipinos, Subic parents have become also ardently persevering in making their children attain education at the college level, at the most, or secondary level, at the least.

Primarily because of poverty, not every child born in the Philippines is known to be able to finish secondary education. This notwithstanding, the degree of literacy in the Philippines on the whole has remained one of the highest, by world standards.

Schooling Equivalency

The national education system of the Philippines was established by and patterned after that of the U.S. One marked difference, though, is that in the U.S. students go through twelve grade levels to finish elementary and secondary education: grade levels 1-6 for elementary, and 7-12 for secondary (grade levels 7-8 are for junior high school and 9-12, senior high school). Thus, with a student's one school year in kindergarten and four school years in college counted, he or she needs a total of seventeen schooling years in a lifetime to attain a bachelor's degree in the U.S., figured thus: 1 year in kinder + 6 years in elementary + 2 years in junior high + 4 years in senior high + 4 years in college = 17 years.

The equivalency of this compared to what obtains in the Philippines sees an academic standard construable as 12% higher in terms of curricular coverage and training period, figured thus: 17 years— 15 years = 2 years, divided by 17 years x (100) = 12%.

This difference stems from the fact that—unlike in the U.S.—students in the Philippines, since 1945, go through a total of only ten school years to finish both elementary and secondary education, i.e., 6 years for elementary and four years for high school equals ten years. Thus, by comparison, a student's attainment of a bachelor's degree in the Philippines normally requires a total of only 15 schooling years in a lifetime, calculated thus: 1-school year stay in kindergarten + 6 years in elementary + 4 years in high school + 4 years in college = 15 years—a period two years less than in the U.S., not only in scholastic preparation period but also in purpose.

Although students' standard attendance period is 200 days per school year (rounded) in the Philippines as against exactly 180 days in the U.S., still, for total amount of time normally required to attain a kindergarten-to-college education, this standard is comparatively lower by 2%, to wit: In the Philippines, 15 school years x 200 days per school year = 3,000 school days; in the U.S., 17 school years x 180 days per school year = 3,060 days; 3,060 school days in the U.S.—3,000 school days in the Philippines = 60 school days difference; 60 school days divided by 3,060 school days = 0.0196; and 0.0196 x 100 =1.96%, rounded to 2%.

Helping Enhance Learning Performance

By all the foregoing differences, as well as by quality of classroom instruction and such other socio-economic conditions that relate to education, it has become common knowledge that teaching-learning performances enjoy generally higher levels in the U.S. than in the Philippines. Cognizant of this, a purely voluntary lecturer once discussed with students in the Subic National High School in 2002 a particular learning motivation-geared lesson, outlined as follows" (aim is essentially to preclude any self-reference).

For lack of an assembly hall, two successive days of pre-scheduled sessions of 15-20 minutes each were held, whereby multi-sectioned 2nd year students were first reminded that they are in school for no other purpose than to achieve their own good future in life. Then they were made to get a clear grasp of how their day-to-day routines or established habits of attentive listening, reading, etc. could in effect enable them—as sure consequence—to earn for their future an income. He calculated that they would gain $105.00 for every hour that they learned from their class work—or lose the same amount forever for every hour they did not learn.

This particular lesson consisted essentially of the following step-by-step mathematical computations/explanations interspersed with relevant food for thought:

1) If a student attains, say, a B.S. degree in the U.S. for a career, average annual income for it could reach $48,000.00 (equivalent to $4,000.00 a month or even more on a case-to-case basis), so that a 40-year lasting career would see a total income of $1,920,000.00, computed thus: $48,000.00 per school year x 40 years = $1,920,000.00.

2) The (arbitrary) figure "40 years" comes from the assumption that a student who starts schooling at 6 in kindergarten and progressively continues up to college could expect to graduate with a four-year B.S. degree at 23, and thereafter embark on a 40-year work span by retiring at 63—which makes for a work span of 40 years because 63— 23 = 40.

3) A total of 18,360 effective-learning hours (via attentive listening, reading, etc.) are required for a $1,920,000.00-envisioned future of any student, and computation is 17 schooling years (pertinently based on the foregoing figures or 17 school years x 180 days per school year = 3,060 school days) x 6 hours per school day = 18,360 hours.

4) Dividing $1,920,000.00 by 18,360 hours = $104.58 per hour or $105.00 (rounded to nearest dollar)—a quotient that calculatedly represents a student's income earned for his/her future, only under instances of "effective learning."

5) This very same supposedly, just-for-illustration "learning income" of $105.00 per hour of students for their future becomes an automatic loss forever in any instance that they do not learn in class at all.

6) The loss is sure to arise because students not learning at all could not be expected consequently to pass tests normally required for getting any $48,000.00-a-year job in the U.S. or anywhere else.

7) It is of paramount importance, therefore, that any student exerts utmost efforts—never hesitating to ask for teachers' help or guidance as needed—in learning, by every possible means, intended lessons for every kind of class work assigned in school—if he/she at all is to have a better opportunity for achieving a good future.

Motivational Lesson's Effect

No less than the principal of the school, Felita C. Pullido, Ed. D., as well as its science teacher, Cecilia Evalles, was appreciative of the lecturer's volunteered service. To both, as were other Subic school principals, were also voluntarily handed out copies of an educational material (Appendix E) with contents deemed quite academically beneficial to ambitious students. In January 2005, the material's educational value apparently found resonance right with the Bureau of Public Schools at Iba, Zambales, so that no less than its Superintendent's Office, thru its Assistant Superintendent Eclar, exerted efforts to disseminate the hand out.

"Golden Age" of National Education

As reported by national media, the ongoing quality of classroom instruction in the Philippines leaves much to be desired. Admittedly, present-day totality of available educational resources plays a very significant role. But if there is any single factor that could incontrovertibly help bring about the most consequential effect in this regard, it is teachers' professional competence. This includes not only subject-matter proficiency but also ability to conduct young, malleable minds towards propensities for purposeful, self-motivated learning. Teachers' proficiency needs to be coupled with parents' own influence and guidance at home to shape a society's young to a future of meeting desired standards.

An episode in Philippine history proves and substantiates this. English was made the medium of instruction, and Filipino stayed the national language in the Philippines. The country's "golden age of education," i.e., the period of a vaunted high-quality school teaching and learning, loomed in the national scene between the years 1901-1941. It was promoted from 1901 on by the "Thomasites"—or groups of American teachers sent to the Philippines by the U.S. government to help in the education of post-Spanish regime Filipinos—a task initiated by the U.S. Army in Corregidor. Primarily because of the Thomasite teachers' contribution to Philippine education, the third largest English-speaking country in world—the Philippines itself—was to later come into being. And primarily because of this factual attribute, too, Filipinos have now become the first choice in most venues of global employment.

Within the period started by the "Thomasites" until 1941, there was in Subic, with its relatively few families, only one public elementary school, which by law was—as it is to this day—free to all. Headed by a lone principal and manned by up to sixteen "municipal teachers" whose salaries averaged only some P60.00 a month but regarded already substantial at the time, the school provided compulsory education for primary and intermediate students in grades 1-7 only. All its classes comprised a student population (with upward trend) of more than 200 that came from different barrios including Balaybay, which later became a part of the town of Castillejos, birthplace of one of the Philippines' most beloved past presidents, Ramon Magsaysay.

Named Subic Elementary School, it stood with a two-storey building painted green (interpreted as symbol of a plant under cultivation for its future yield) and was standard-dimensioned and located at the town's central area. Instructional devices and resource materials were not profuse, but teachers' sheer proficiency and competence created reputations giving justice to 4th-5th graders' priding themselves—in their later years—on their being already skilled with mathematical problems involving fractions, decimals, and percentages. It also became a mark of distinctive academic achievement among seventh graders of the time that most of them proved already qualified to teach—with a government summer school in Baguio, aside from the Philippine Normal School in Manila, serving as a vehicle for their professional upgrading. For those in quest of further education, on the other hand, a trade school in Iba, the capital of Zambales, was a favored oasis, and this was because of its widely known teachings of readily job-applicable trade and industrial arts, skills-rich courses in carpentry, woodcraft, rattan craft, etc.

Factors of Productive Teaching

Mainly, three major factors are seen to have significantly accounted for the era's vaunted A-1 quality of teachers' input of classroom tutelage, on one hand, and students' illustrious lesson assimilation as output, on the other. First was institution of a norm of intensive 200-day curriculum geared towards mastery of the three "R's" (reading, arithmetic, and writing), as well as teaching of well-planned lessons in English, geography, and other subjects that lent immediate practical applicability. The principal established high goals. To cite just a particular actual instance, to hone primary students' reading proficiency, he conducted oral reading tests periodically during pre-scheduled classroom visitations. By this kind of concern exercised on behalf of the young, graduating seventh graders' overall training proved quite effective for pursuit of further education or for outright embarkation on homemaking or income-earning handicraft applications—like sewing, drafting, etc.

Second was teachers' practice of corporal punishment as means of instilling proper discipline among students. As a fact that speaks for itself, this is hardly deniable with respect to—not considering its total inadvisability for understandable reasons—its contributory effect, to a certain extent, in the conditioning of students into becoming better learners.

And third was non-existence yet of such personal entertainment-geared but study-detracting electronics gadgetry and devices, as TV, Nintendo, Walkman radios, etc., which are distracting in today's quickly modernizing countries as remarkable fruitions of advances in technology.

If there is any other particularly palpable reflection of the superior quality of grade-school education in Subic at the time, it was about an amazing student band. As part of their civics studies and arts projects, sixth and seventh graders once held a town parade, using a band for which they had crafted all of its musical instruments mainly out of bohos under the direction of the ingenious teachers at the time.

None is seen, however, to be a more eloquent indication of what is central in this regard than the fact that teachers responsible for it all were mostly not in possession of B.S. degrees, but only education through seventh grade. These teachers underwent professional upgrading while in service or through schematic internships.

Decline and Rehabilitation of Education in Subic

In late 1941, the glow of light that Subic's public education had for its saplings just suddenly darkened with a three-year literacy derailment. Its lone public school was one of some targets unexpectedly bombed by Japanese planes before noon of Sunday, December 8, 1941—one fateful moment, indeed, of the onset of the Pacific War. As the bomb used was non-incendiary but of a demolition kind, only the middle, staired, frontal part of the school, which was wholly a wooden structure, was wrecked. Thus, when Japanese conquerors needed to garrison themselves in Subic later, the school's undamaged rooms, which had a corridor stocked up with some saved, negligibly shrapnel-scathed desks, were made use of; but it simply was for forced teaching of pupils at the time. As war-bred doubts, uncertainties, and suspicions soaked interactions among the conquered and the conquerors in Subic, not counting cruel outcomes of surveillance by the Kempetai (Japanese secret police) with some local collaborators' connivance, public education administered by the latter was anything but inspiring.

Puppet Government's Decoy for Subiquenians' Allegiance with Japan

By what actually was foisted off as a doctrine of a better tomorrow via the slogan "Greater Asia Co-Prosperity Sphere," the ruling authorities tried to re-orient peoples' minds on, if not brainwash them into, what was coined and dished out as "Kalibapi," meaning "Kalayaang Independente ng Bagong Pilipinas." It meant in English, "Independent Freedom for a New Philippines." For calculated effect, the sole high-profile Filipino expatriate in Japan, General Artemio Ricarte alias "Vibora" who remained steadfast with his opposition to the U.S. as was General Emilio Aguinaldo at first, was made to appear in public meetings aimed at trumpeting out Kalibapi's purported benefits to Filipinos. Also, laborers employed by the Japanese in the Subic Bay Naval Base were even bowed to (saluted) by soldier-sentries whenever seen wearing on their chests ID cards frontally emblazoning the word "**Kalibapi.**" In addition, as another way of propagating in Filipinos' psyche what supposedly could be the onset of better times under Japanese rule, a cigarette labeled with the brand name "Kalibapi" started appearing in stores. But these Japanese motivation-rich gestures actually resonated with only a tiny fraction of Subic's citizens—and they were mostly those called "Makapili"—the equivalent of "Quislings"—as best exemplified by General Ricarte himself. Thus, the ruling enemy's attempt to rehabilitate Subic's war-retarded public education amid its lack of concern for improving other aspects of town folks' living conditions, according as its empty rhetoric purported to envision, only ended in vain. It was actually only after U.S. Liberation came that Subic's public education—and other needs for normal community living—enjoyed an opportunity for a new start again. Solely for the matter of education, post-war reparations combined with government cash outlays gradually effected improvements needed in Subic's new program and infrastructure for the educational upbringing of its young.

Present Educational Growth

Today, 65 years after the Philippines' gained of independence on July 4, 1946, in Subic there are twenty-one complete public elementary schools, including one primary school and the Special Education Center for the Gifted at Ilwas Elementary School, jointly adopted by the Josephine F. Khonghun Foundation and the Local Government of Subic headed by Municipal Mayor, Hon. Jeffrey D. Khonghun, four public high schools, one public college, and a number of private pre-schools, elementary, and secondary schools. Subic's first and oldest high school is private and church-connected. It is called Saint James School, which was founded in 1945 as Saint James High School, and named after the town's patron saint. It was followed by the establishment years later of the Saint Anthony's High School, also private and church-managed. The older of the town's two public high schools, now called Subic High School, saw initial operations in 1987. The second Subic public high school established is named Cawag High School and was established in 1992. Appendix F tabulates Subic's schools and their respective latest enrollment, faculty size, and administrators, under public and private categories.

In the annals of public education in Subic, some particular epochal occurrences of a province-wide, if not nationwide, significance had taken place in recent years. Mainly, this is because of understandable ends pursued by all of the educators involved, in their capacity as either an administrator or plain faculty member. As per Joint Circular No. 1, series 1998, issued by DECS, DBM and DILG, provides the payment of existing allowances of teachers in the amount of P200.00 granted by Local Government Unit (LGU) chargeable against Special Education Fund (SEF) as of December 31, 1997 and that, any additional allowances granted to teachers by LGUs are charged to the general fund of LGUs subject to the existing budgeting rules and regulations.

Another epoch-making achievement in the realm of education in Subic is the networking and social advocacy among the Department of Education (DepEd) personnel, Local Government officials, Non-Government Units (NGOs) and the townspeople. This came about as a result of circumstantially warranted, innovative measures instituted by the Subic School District Office, which is currently headed by Madam Amelia H. Mojica, D. Ed., as supervisor.

MUNICIPAL ECONOMY

Annual Revenue

Subic's economy as a municipality has grown quite robustly over the past three years. With a total workforce of only 211 in 2002 harnessed for its normal upkeep and dispensation of essential services to the community, this has grown to 273 in 2005. Based on figures supplied—at an interview-necessitated instruction of Subic Sanggunian Bayan Secretary Eva D. Bertes—by Municipal Budget Officer Emma Quintos, Subic chalked up revenues totaling P88,313,672.69 in 2005. This is 34% more than the town's total income of P66,141,073.61 in 2002. Variously sourced taxes and fees and a 1% share (runs to P4-P5 million) from the Subic Bay Metropolitan Authority constitute the bulk of the town's municipal income.

Public Market

One of the most reliable sources of Subic's municipal income with respect to payment certainty and regularity is the town's public market. From originally being a shed-like building with only some six walled stalls and several open, long tables for merchandize display until the 1960s, the market, originally located at where the new municipal hall now stands, has evolved into the multi-stalled configuration and dimension it has today—on a site that was once a shore. Annual receipts from the expanded market (by more than three times the floor area of its predecessor) run to more than P2 million, but this is dwarfed by municipal licenses or business taxes, which are paid as well by market stall holders. For 2005, nearly P12.90 million, inclusive of payment receipts from other businesses not housed in the market, was realized from municipal licenses.

Peacetime Economic Conditions

Generally, economic conditions in Subic before the Pacific War assumed a three-tiered description, capsulated in the sense of one characterizing just a few families as with resources of more than enough; most, just enough; and some, hardly enough. The town as a whole thrived primarily on fishing, farming, and (small-scale) logging. Families not engaged in these chief means of livelihood depended on employment in private and public establishments. Mainly, these establishments included the Subic municipal office, and the town's only public school, the U.S. Navy shipyard in Olongapo, and a road maintenance office with a group of camineros (road workers), and a lone transportation company called Try-Tran that was owned by the famous Filipino philanthropist, Teodoro R. Yangco of the town of San Antonio.

Other families carried on enterprises with limited competition, which, among other businesses like tiendas, garment stores, pork-beef market stalls, bakeshops, etc., included only one gas station, one hardware store, one pharmacy, one restaurant, one refreshment parlor, one barbershop, one apparel shop, and a lone mineral-water distributor (with the trade name "Vida Salud"). Also, cottage industries like salt making, "bagoong" (fish sauce) making, sewing, cake making, blacksmithing, sausage making, etc. were engaged in among neighborhoods. Then for breadwinners who could not find jobs to levels of their qualifications, serving as "jueteng" (wagered numbers game for multiplied prizes) collectors was an expediently last recourse for making a living.

The non-sophisticated nature yet of life's ways during the time made simple living the norm of families' day-to-day activities. Except in offices, people moved about in town even with only wooden shoes, and the wearing of "kalapyaw" (or poncho) made of palms was an ordinary sight on rainy days. Minimum wage bordered on only P2.00 a day, but population density, as pitted against means to support it was not yet a problem, thereby making the amount fairly commensurate with what was essential for most families' economic normalcy. Electricity was just hoped for at the time, but, still, life even without it somehow went on with all simplicity—and most Subic folks simply felt generally satisfied with their lot under the time's economic standards—not engaging in the sort of street marches characterizing the trends of the present era.

Wartime Economy, Recovery, and Prosperity

If there was any time in Subic when its resources, including its people, were haplessly exploited under a total loss of all that goes with human freedom just for satisfaction of a ruling authority's sustained dominance over its subjects, it set in when Subic was ruled by a detachment of Japanese soldiers during the Pacific War. For three years town folks were pervasively unhappy because of hardships of making ends meet as result of the unexpected ravages of war. Their most difficult times took place as they resettled their homes back from evacuation in the mountains when the enemy invaders moved in to occupy the town. Debilitating disease caused by mosquitoes and unsafe water in the mountains, on one hand, and hunger resulting from lack of food in the market, on the other, grimly stalked Subic and its vicinities. Fear and mistrust of the enemy bogged almost every economic activity down to a virtual standstill, with farm production being carried on only to a self-subsistence extent. Mickey Mouse money was later procedurally made to abound, but it all remained useless against the scarcity of food for the hungry and the dearth of medicines for the sick. For sheer want and helplessness, people who needlessly died at the wrong time were in most cases just immediately buried—with mats wrapped around corpses serving as their very coffins. The plight of people's extreme suffering from the dehumanizing throes of hunger was such that even the pulp or residue of already chewed-up sugarcane thrown on the street would be picked up and re-chewed by some gaunt, greatly emaciated figures—whose appearance was reminiscent of prisoners in Nazi interment camps, with garments worn being only the mark of difference. Among many malnourished children and even adults, puffed-up feet and legs called "manas" ("edema" in English) became a common sight for some time.

As medicines could hardly be availed of anywhere, and only herbs and roots were used for cures, those who came through Subic's wartime conditions were to later share a common belief: they were survivors not only of the Pacific War itself, but were the fittest victors as well of a struggle that was in a way relatively more testy—what with just their genetic mettle serving as their sole source of defensive weaponry.

If Subic's overall suffering as a community of actually peace-loving people ended at last, it came so only because of General Douglas MacArthur's success in fulfilling his promise, "I shall return!" to the Filipinos when the Philippines fell to Japanese hands in 1942. Upon Subic's liberation in 1945 by American GIs who met excited crowds' multi-gestured greetings of a long-awaited welcome which occasionally saw stoning of Japanese POWs on trucks even as their American captors protectively shielded them by hand, pervasive euphoria engulfed the whole town. Spirited speculations spawned by a sort of an economically uplifting windfall from money-generating ventures gained footholds in most of Subic's households. As seen in practically every nook and corner of Subic, abruptly repaired and renovated homes or portions of them were transformed into bars, nightclubs, and restaurants, with live music and crooners. Many American GI groups in battle outfits, who now and then took breaks from their nearby encampments, profusely spent both U.S. currency coins and "Victory" stamped Philippine peso bills for their good times, while songs like "You Are My Sunshine," "I Walk Alone," "You'll Never Know," "Roll Out the Barrel," etc., filled the air. Of the time's scenario, "Subic never had it so good in business, indeed!" was what in essence cropped up in most people's thoughts. But none remained more pertinent than the fact that for all that Subic underwent in the Pacific War, it now found itself, after all the years that followed, socio-economically benefitting from where it is today—an episode of its own history as inarguably begun by the once-famed Subic Bay U.S. Naval Base. It was what bestowed the main strength of Subic's economy for years then—and to a point that gradually saw the town's former Barrio, Olongapo, become a city.

Naval Facility's Other Side Economic Effects

Actually, employment was not the only economic opportunity created in the course of the operations of Subic Bay U.S. Naval Facility. Road and building construction-related businesses also laid open doors for private entities' opportunity to forge big-time contracts on bilaterally agreed-upon transactions with U.S. Navy authorities. In 1964, a business couple, Alfredo and Lucia Viacrusis, started a trucking enterprise in Subic that supplied concrete aggregates to infrastructure contractors in the U.S. Naval Base. After 13 years, they reorganized their business by putting up the Rocky Mountain Construction Corporation (RMCC), with management being entrusted to their children. By acquiring from the U.S. a 100-ton-per-hour asphalt plant, and erecting it in Subic in 1981, the RMCC managed to supply and lay out asphalt concrete on roads, runways, and parking areas in and off the U.S. Naval Base at competitive prices. The company's acquisition of other kinds of equipment led to expansion of its operations. It managed to successfully branch out to earthmoving, concrete paving work, etc.

In 1995, with the U.S. Navy no longer in Subic, the RMCC upgraded its operations by engaging in a two-pronged thrust into the construction business wherein one company division took care of earthmoving, concrete paving, and structuring buildings, while the other concentrated on the marketing of rock crusher products, ready-mixed concrete supply, asphalt concrete, asphalt paving, and equipment rental.

Many other business enterprises even of smaller scale had thrived lucratively in Subic over time, despite the U.S. Navy's departure from Subic in the 1990s. Mainly, they are in the nature of shell crafts, concrete products, iron works, garment making, and the culturing of crabs, prawns, shells, and milkfish in an area of more than 200 hectares of riverbanks and shorelines.

Improvements in Economic Facilities

Until the 1970s, water supply for home use was a great problem in Subic. As solution, Municipal Resolution No.19 was passed, establishing the Subic Water District under the provisions of PD 198 (Provincial Water Utilities Act of 1973). Subject to corporate rules and regulations under the administration of LWUA as a regulatory body, it was initially managed by former Subic Municipal Counselor Isaias Vindua, who had retired from the entity in the early 2000s.

Electricity, an all-important commodity that became available in Subic for the first time in 1945, has also now become available town wide among most homes in Subic around the clock. The National Power Corporation supplies it through the Zambales Electric Cooperative II, which was formed on October 25, 1984. By its good record and performance, the coop received the Best Electric Coop Award in Region III from 1987-1991. It is known that the coop exemplarily progressed under the management of Angel G. Laureano from 1989 to 1997. About 96% of homes in Subic are estimated to be currently with electricity under the coop's services.

The Wawandue Fish Port, Inc., established and registered with the Philippine Securities and Exchange Commission (SEC) in mid-1990, is also one of the mainstays of Subic's present-day economy, for it has since been significantly benefitting fishermen and fish consumers alike in practically the entire province of Zambales. Although a company engaged primarily in commercial fishing, it carries on as well ice production and cold storage operations of province-wide coverage. It started large-scale operations under the management of Jeffrey D. Khonghun, who became municipal mayor in 2001.

For the town's expanded needs for telecommunications and postal services, the Bureau of Telecommunications (BUTEL) and the Philippine Postal Authority are known to be up to standards. Aside from these two government agencies, there is the PILTEL that caters to long-distance local and international telephone calls and the LBC, to mail and cargo deliveries, both on domestic and global scales.

Four private banks operate currently in Subic, namely: Metrobank, Progress Bank, San Marcelino Bank, and Bataan Savings Bank. Other commercial establishments that gradually came into being one after the other and somehow contributed to Subic's marked burgeoning within the last two decades are the Larkin Leather Bag Company, Benguet Mining Corporation, Pacific Rare Metals, Inc., and CATV.

The rise in Subic's population is partly due to other variously growing businesses.

Transients' need for accommodations resultantly gave rise to growth of subdivisions, not to mention some houses for rent, over the years. Subic's five major subdivisions are the Sta. Monica Subdivision, St. Theodore Subdivision, the Executive Village, St. James Subdivision, Subic Homes, Subic Hills Village, Villa Venezia, WEA Homes, and Maligaya Village. For low-salaried municipal employees, Subic Mayor Khonghun is known to be currently planning a low-cost housing project.

Expatriates' Hand in the Local Economy

To an undetermined extent, the overall economic progress prevailing in Subic today is partly attributable to dollar remittances to families made by their foreign-based relatives—in the U.S., Middle East, etc. This is particularly true of cases where recipients are circumstantially incapable of joining and living with their supporting relatives abroad.

But cash donations are also sent from abroad on occasion to certain Subic establishments. One actual case is a $3,500.00 check (equivalent to some

P189, 000.00) sent in on 2005 to the Saint James School (SJS) by the Subic Association of San Diego, California (its president of the time was Subiquenian USN retiree, Andrew Dalopo). The amount was actually received by the school but ultimately paid in full to the contractor of its fence renovation project. The donation was made through the contractor's father's pre-arrangements and representations in person with the Subic-based school and the donor association in California. The Saint James School was made recipient of the donation because, as honoree, it is the beloved alma mater of about four hundred fifty alumni that gathered on July 23, 2005, at the plush Suncoast Hotel-Casino, Las Vegas, Nevada, in a reunion/commemoration of its 60th Founding Anniversary (since its establishment in 1945).

For all the anticipation associated with a once-in-sixty-years reunion for being seen and seeing others again in a high-class venue, each participant paid $75.00—exclusive of hotel accommodations and other incidental costs. Net of all expenses and of the $3,500.00-cash donation to the Saint James School, remaining surplus was some $11,000.00—as learned from a phone interview. But the question of who owns this surplus fund—for all that it represents to date—has become a matter of debate, if not of controversy. One run of thought is that the alumni association of the Saint James School has the right of ownership for it. On the other hand, the Subic Association of San Diego maintains a similar claim, on grounds of its own part as an instrumentality, too, for the realization of the fund. How a commonality of thoughts can be achieved is unknown.

Highlighted—after a traditional Thanksgiving Mass—with reunion socials, gala night, dinner, dance, etc., the celebration culminated in "a great fun for everyone." But it was not necessarily coordinated, managed, or controlled by any individual person or any California-based Saint James School alumni association. Instead, reported as largely responsible was a 24-member, "all-alumni committee"—whose work was coordinated through and with the help of the Subic Association of San Diego, an organization with members understood to comprise Subiquenians living in San Diego (Annex G presents the 2005 affair's jointly responsible alumni-association officers—as shown in the souvenir program for it).

Coordination of the affair was effected through phone calls and the Internet. As cash needed to be deposited with the venue hotel at Las Vegas for the reservation, some of the reunion organizers had to advance payment out of their own pockets first. Afterwards, they were reimbursed their expenses. As is made known, whatever decisions the association makes in conducting its affairs is understood to be solely within its own domain as an association, not within the purview of any other entity's concerns. The fact that the association's treasurer is reputably financially well off, being an owner-operator of four Subway restaurants as a franchise holder, somehow helps a lot in preserving trust in all of its fund-raising activities. She is responsible only for her money custodial functions, however, and does not have anything to do whatsoever with decision-making involving association fund utilization. Since its existence, the association claims to have been donating a part of the funds it periodically raises for its Subic Saint James School scholarship program, regardless of its other civic projects.

Actually, the other Subicquenian associations formed not only in California but also other parts of the U.S.—if only for the exercise of civic-mindedness—could well lend a hand, directly or indirectly, in furthering Subic's socio-economic growth. Practically all appear dedicated to the pursuit of unity via even their founding provisions and common associational amenities and other social niceties displayed, if not necessarily role-modeled, by their officers. But this—in all reality—is deemed true and existent only, if at all, where there are no instances of arrogance-bred pataasan-/inggitan-/dunungan or pakitang-tao-lamang actions, or stewardship by officers perceived to be in close kinship or engaged in occupational lines quite palpably dependent only on people connections of sizable proportions. And while there are undeniably other U.S.-based Pinoy associations that appear really worth taking pride in to be affiliated with by virtue of their exemplary civic undertakings, only the Subic Association of San Diego so far appears to remain a pace setter among Subiquenian expatriates in this regard. Since its existence, it spearheads and takes charge of the holding of a Subic fiesta in San Diego, not mentioning other worthy civic activities it professes to undertake.

Tourism Establishments

As a coastal town frequented by weekend tourists on group excursions from as far as Manila and neighboring provinces of hinterland locations, i.e., without shores, Subic—exclusive of the SBMA complex's interiors and vicinities, boasts of a total of ten major beach resorts: Subic Beach, Club Morocco Hotel and Beach Resort (formerly La Sirena), Roma's Beach, Green Beach, Miami Beach, Pamana Island Resort (Snake Island), AL Beach, La Playa Beach, Paradise Beach, and White Rock Quality Hotel and Beach Resort.

All these beach resorts are frequented as well by tourists from other parts of the world. Most are Filipino pensioners from the U.S. who were once with the U.S. Navy or army. Others come from Europe, the U.S. Australia, China, Japan, and Korea, on the main.

Actually, the name, "Snake Island," as applied to the Pamana Beach Resort, came into usage not for any reason having to do with snakes; instead, the island, which poses a "really scenic," eye-catching view within a distance of about half a mile from Subic town's nearest point, was said to be a favorite rendezvous where lovers used to "sneak" to on weekends. The fact that Subiquenians' accent makes pronunciation of "sneak" sound like "snake" has accounted for the use and staying of the (pronounced) name, "Snake Island."

Other Indicators of Economic Progress

The strength of a town's economy is somehow reflected in the scope of basic health care services that are made available for its population. All in all, there are today in Subic more than 100 health-care workers in ten medical clinics, two barangay health stations, some ten dental clinics, one social-hygiene clinic and one rural health unit. This statistical information simply speaks of a gigantic stride in the matter of health as a municipal concern for Subic's citizens, who, in the past, used to enjoy, until the 1980s, the services of only one physician and one nurse for their immediate free health-care attention.

Poverty still exists among some families in Subic—just as it incontrovertibly does anywhere in the world, but the fact that most are in a relatively better economic shape today could hardly be denied. In the past, walking among the great majority of Subic citizens was a necessity when going to church, school, or market; but now, reliance on multi-form transportation including tricycles, if not pedal cabs, has become a more common luxury. Also, time was when most have-nots would go to houses of the haves to watch favorite television shows; today, almost every home has its own electronic entertainment set. And then, where before, most families lacked telephones as a sort of home necessity, now most average families possess phones and even the luxury of cell phones. Furthermore, computerization and other forms of technological modernity appear growing to such extent that equating this with zero prosperity is simply being blind to reality. Even just for all these as typical hallmarks of economic progress,

Subic folks could only appear as generally having now achieved, indeed, a level of sophisticated living, no longer what those of the past used to satisfy themselves with: just a simple day-to-day living.

TOWN'S PEACE AND ORDER CONDITIONS

Subic is an urban town where peace and order have remained generally satisfactory. The only post-war time when community security warranted particularly around-the-clock alertness for dangers from potential troublemakers occurred after the Philippines' gain of independence in 1946. Remnants of the "Hukbalahap" ("Hukbong Bayan Laban sa Hapon") or "Forces Against Japanese," in English, reorganized themselves into a group that they renamed "Hukbong Magpapalaya ng Bayan" or "Forces for Peoples' Freedom" in English translation, and chose to go underground for what they deemed as still-unresolved tenancy problems they had with their landlords. At that period Philippine Constabulary (PC) forces were stationed as a full company in Subic from 1946 until the 1950s. With headquarters at Mangan-vaca, they were separate from a (PC) force that was stationed in Maquinaya, where a checkpoint periodically operated.

Today, Subic has problems of its own that are related to common crimes like robbery, thievery, substance trafficking, etc. But the situation appears under normal control of the Subic Philippine National Police, presently headed by Chief Superintendent Cesar Jacob.

MUNICIPAL GOVERNMENT AND POLITICS

Administrative Set-Up

The management and control—as in other Philippine towns—of the machinery of Subic's governmental affairs operate in two levels: municipal and barangay. At the municipal level the governing body is an administrative group headed by the municipal mayor—with a vice-mayor, eight Sanggunian Bayan members (or councilors), and other officials comprising the rest in subordinate capacities.

As of March 2007, Subic's municipal affairs are administered by the following officials:

Elected Group

Jeffrey D. Khonghun—Municipal Mayor
Lauro B. Simbol—Municipal Vice Mayor
Reynaldo S. dela Cruz—Municipal Councilor
Pedro F. Delgado—Municipal Councilor
Juan R. Deveraturda III—Municipal Councilor
Jose B. Felarca—Municipal Councilor
Danilo F. Fontelera—Municipal Councilor
Ruben Gaduang—Municipal Councilor
Leonardo L. Gonzales—Municipal Councilor
Leonardo O. Guevara, Jr.—Municipal Councilor
Ricardo L. Cabal—ABC Federation President
Michael Angelo K. Ting—SK Federation President

Appointed Group

Eva D. Bertes—Sangguniang Bayan Secretary
Ricardo F. Otero, Jr.—Municipal Secretary
Sonia B. Doble—Municipal Treasurer
Emma A. Quintos—Budget Officer
Juliet T. Mercado—Accounting Officer
Sylvia DG. Magno—Municipal Assessor
Noel M. Solano—Municipal Engineer
Genaro Ramoso, Ph. D.—Planning & Development Officer
Leonardo F. Afable, MD—Municipal Health Officer
Arcella Demitita—Municipal Agricultural Officer
Jaime Reguerra—Local Civil Registrar
Nellie D. Pagar—Municipal Social Welfare Officer
Illuminada Lopez—Human Resource Officer

At the barangay level, on the other hand, functions an administrating body headed by the barangay or barrio captain—with eight Sanggunian Barangay members (or "kagawads"), a secretary-treasurer, and some barangay tanods (or barrio guards) as the rest of the body. Except barrio guards, all officials in both the municipal and the barangay levels get entrusted with their respective posts by election, and they all get paid from government funds.

As of March 2007, Subic's baranggay captains, by barrio, are all named below:

Aningway-Sacatihan—Cesar E. Antonio
Asinan-Poblacion—Rogelio M. Cabral
Asinan-Proper—Jose E. Calderon
Baraca-Camachile—Presita S. dela Paz
Batiawan—Jesus S. Dizon
Capapacuan—Nelson B. Coil
Calapandayan—Ruel P. Sarmiento
Cawag—Leonardo A. Adorna
Ilwas—Ariel R. Apostol
Mangan-Vaca—Eduarte F. Agoyaoy
Matain—Leonardo M. Villar
Naugsol—Flora C. Mayo
Pamatawan—Rodolfo A. Agustin
San Isidro—Flocerfida L. Bobis
Santo Tomas—Ricardo L. Cabal
Wawandue—an M. Novales

Although it appears to belong to the lowest rung of a municipal government's ladder of political power, being a barangay captain has become since the 1950s a tightly raced-for position in Subic.

Unlike in certain organizations where names could just be listed in ballots for voters' election of officers whose true intentions are compromised by a schematic, one-sided design to ensure emergence of a pre-decided winner, anyone desiring to become a barrio captain in Subic entails a high cost today. Also, where in past years when only a few hardly minded the position's importance, the other way around has now taken hold of many politically inclined individuals' minds. Regardless of the position's projection of social prestige, two other motivating factors have become strongly associated with it: political power and financial remuneration. This is to such extent that candidates had admitted to having spent substantial sums campaigning for it. And what had proven to be more concern-evoking among prospective seekers of the position are certain risks involved, even if right the electorate's own interests are what a candidate aims to serve—as a necessary means of winning in an election.

A typical case in point was about how a certain barangay captain candidate in Subic's Barangay Sto. Tomas was reportedly murdered on May 3, 1997, simply "because he stood in the way of a higher political leader's desire to own a piece of land that the victim had helped get individually registered by parcels in the names of its small occupants who were from his political bailiwick." The case underwent court litigation and national multi-media exposure in detail, so that almost everyone in Subic realized how political power entrusted in wrong hands could be used to satisfy one's greed via brazen use of government resources in a modus operandi smacking only of a dreaded Mafia style.

New Norm of Office Conduct

New, unprecedented routines go with the way Subic governmental affairs are run today.

With high approbation, it hardly escaped people's perception even on the very start of the first-time aldermanship of incumbent Mayor Jeffrey D. Khonghun, following the 2001 mayoral election. Regardless of all municipal facilities or services Subic folks have since been enjoying—which are somehow ascribable to past and succeeding local administrations, anyway, it is the mayor's yet-to-be equaled institution of a tightly adhered-to norm of conduct and discipline among officials and the rank-and-file alike that people particularly resonate with. In a nutshell, what any visitor is most likely to get impressed with once his or her purpose gets served in any office at the Subic Municipal Hall would be about the thought that it is not, after all, always dirty in Philippine politics or the government—a conclusion most likely to develop in one's mind, as if by dictate of endless hope, out of the age-old Filipino observation, "Graft and corruption is an ordinary occurrence in the realm of public service in the Philippines." Put simply, officials and rank-and-file alike appear to agree that office conduct should be more integrity-conscious, rather than duty-oblivious.

And gone, too, are the likes of "actual happenings in the past where, chiefly because of glaringly indefensible itemizations or pricings for structural bills of materials, even a newly hired engineer thought it better to resign his municipal position, rather than be a pressured party to a transaction certifiable as bona fide only via his signature, regardless of the importance, too, of proper bidding."

Indeed, from the way those presently in the service of Subic's municipal government go about in their work—apparently by virtue of Mayor

Khonghun's own established mode of administrative leadership—are favorably created impressions tending to erase the past's bad shadows cast by the aforesaid realities. Thus, it may yet be shown and proven right in Subic itself that not all Filipino politicians are what they have become customarily seen by the general public—and that in any human endeavor where aim is essentially for the general weal of all, what fundamentally counts is always attributable to a leader holding the helm that steers such endeavor. By a paraphrase, this is expressible thus: "It all depends upon a singer, not a song." And this simply implies that people always tend to applaud a singer for an attribute of voice or style, not necessarily for melody or lyrics alone.

"In Philippine politics," a past Subic municipal councilor once said, "there is hardly a treasure of virtue, only just power ever-tending to corrupt the weak-willed, in particular!"

But this appears somehow belied right by the quite palpable example of the way Subic's present Mayor Khonghun is doing his job as both a political leader and a municipal executive. He, in fact, is regarded as a far different singer of the same song all his predecessors had rendered during their own time—public service. This is premised on the parallel idea that in the realm of politics, public service is the very song that political leaders almost always unilaterally render or sing—with themselves naturally judged on the basis not of what they are singing but on that of how they perform. People simply see that Mayor Khonghun's own way of singing or doing his job is what makes a difference: It is not personal aggrandizement but purely expected service to the general public.

Erection of New Municipal Hall

In most respects, the fully air-conditioned concrete building housing the entire Subic municipal government's administrative machinery is quite modern compared with its predecessor. Until 1967, Subic's former Municipal Hall was located in an interior area next to the Roman Catholic Church. Subic's first Municipal Hall was a wooden two-story building believed to be erected in 1910. The building's dilapidation by time necessitated construction not only of a new one but also selection of a new site. The original Subic Public Market was transferred to where it is today, and its resultant vacated space, in turn, is where the new Municipal Hall presently stands. To the PTA of the Subic Central School was then donated the abandoned site of the old Municipal Building.

In an official record under the care of Illuminada Morales-Lopez, Subic Municipal Affairs Officer, it is shown that the erection of the new Municipal Hall began in 1965, and the building was finished in 1967 under the administration of Mayor Dangal Guevara (he had passed away in the late 1990s). Excluding post-1967 renovation and/or expansion cost, expenditures totaled P150, 000.00.

The building came into initial use after the November 1967 national elections. Mayor-elect Guevara and nine other elected officials led a brief inaugural as part of a ceremony ushering in the building's first-time use. From that time on the building underwent staggered renovation and expansion that included its plaza in front. This continued according as municipal funds allowed under the administration—chronologically—of Mayor Dangal Guevara in 1967-1986, Mayor Molina in 1987-1998, Mayor Leonardo Guevara in 1998-2001, and incumbent Mayor Khonghun himself starting in 2001.

Longest Mayoral Reign

Mayor Dangal Guevara stayed the longest in office—total of 18 years. This long tenure is traceable largely to President Ferdinand Marcos' martial-law years. But also instrumental was the mayor's much-vaunted political charisma built out of a widely admired way he dealt with people, be they political allies or foes. One particular thing known most about him was that he knew well how to control and hide his emotion even under situations where only anger could be expected from him in meetings with his fellow municipal officials—and this earned him praises, the most common of which is "mahusay" (or "good"). Another was that whenever one in extreme need approached him for cash help (for medicine, hospital, burial, etc.), he would at times write down a note, take off his watch from his wrist, and then tell the help seeker to go to a big store owner and show the note and the watch for an amount of money afforded.

Because of his reputed popularity with the mass of Subic's electorate, he became the most sought-for political leader among provincial political leaders who needed help in shaping a sure win among them for their respective targeted posts. The fact that all those included in his ticket, from vice-mayor to councilors, always won in practically every past mayoral election held in Subic simply reflects how really popular he was during his political heyday. Another indication relative to this is the fact that his son

Leonardo also became one of Subic's mayors after his demise in the 1990s due to age. Actually, Subic folks attribute his son's becoming a mayor as a gesture of gratitude to his father.

Subic's Post-Marcos Era Politics

It was a general consensus in Subic that had the "1986 People Power" not shoved President Ferdinand Marcos off Philippine politics and ushered in President Corazon Aquino to take his place, Mayor Dangal Guevara would have stayed longer in office. When he did have to vacate his post in the wake of the national government's transition from the political leadership of ousted President Marcos in 1986 to incoming President Aquino, several names of aspirants cropped up for taking over, but with only one would be designated—not by outright election but appointment with necessary pre-endorsements.

By this, petty rivalries, not only among the principal aspirants but also their respective groups or factions of friends started to build up and spawn intrigue—personal and political. In certain instances where word-of-mouth-sown intrigue just burst into the open with heated exchange of accusations and blame, even contemporary friendships and kinships of sorts broke up—with disenchantments being only the ultimate price exacted of all involved, directly or indirectly.

And regardless of whether or not the complete background of all the aspirants—a retired school superintendent, two municipal councilors, a retired bank employee, and a Subic Bay U.S. Naval Base employee—was duly scrutinized, the one deemed the worthiest repository of public trust for "Subic's years ahead" was Manuel Molina, Jr. He was appointed officer-in-charge (OIC) for Subic's vacated mayor's office, with Segundino Sandoval, "balae" of Mayor Guevara, as his vice-OIC.

A Wonder of Municipal Politics

Almost single-handedly, it was Sandoval who helped—in the company of UNIDO politicians, of course—in campaigns against President Marcos during the "snap election" of 1986 in Subic, and it was partly by his representations that he and Molina had teamed up together for heading the 1986-1987 pre-election local government for the town. He first saw active involvement in Subic politics in 1969 when he, together with Polding

Veloria, a former barangay captain of Mangan-Vaca, served as one of a trio of neophytes in local polling result ascertainment. Both of them joined with the coordinator of the Nationalista Party in Subic at the time in recruiting poll watchers arrayed against Mayor Dangal Guevarra's own, in his capacity as head of the opposing Liberal Party. The principal protagonists were then incumbent President Marcos and presidential aspirant Sergio Osmena, Sr. The Nationalista Party municipal coordinator was no less than one of the aspirants for Subic's OIC-mayor in subsequent years, and he was appointed as such by the first-time vice-governor candidate for Zambales, PNB Director Antonio M. Diaz, who was to later become one of Zambales' favorite representatives to congress.

Now, whatever was outgoing Mayor Guevara's role in regard to Sandoval's having later assumed two kinds of leading political posts one after the other with hardly any sign of aspirations for it on his part—a matter necessarily connectible between two "balaes"—has remained only within the domain of pure conjecture. But to most folks in Subic it appeared quite surprisingly significant that Sandoval, who all along had made himself seen as always politically opposed to his balae mayor, had managed to occupy—even only for a very short period—the town's second-highest political post, followed by that for mayor itself. Actually, he was known to have never shown nor expressed even so much as an iota of interest in either of the jobs. And so it was that, among most Subiquenian political observers, the Filipino saying, "Ang kapalaran, 'di mo man hanapin, mapapasa-iyo rin!" ("One's fate, even if not sought for, goes to you somehow in the end!") appeared to have proven true in Sandoval's becoming Subic's vice-mayor. This seemed to be true as well when he became an appointed mayor in 1988, even if only for less than half a year. And on the part of those who aspired for Subic's similar or other political posts but never acquired so unlike in Sandoval's case, on the other hand, was seen a counterpart fulfillment of the relevantly opposite Filipino saying, "Kapalarang 'di ukol, kailan man, 'di bubukol"—or, in English, "Fate not predestined will never emerge!"

A Classic Fruition of Political Adventure

After Manuel Molina, Jr. got appointed mayoral OIC for Subic in 1986, fate saw him achieved thereafter the maximum 12-year tenure allowed by law for elected officials. On the local election of May 13, 1998, statutorily held from remaining permanent mayor, his love for politics made him succeed in seeing himself vice-mayor of mayor-elect Leonardo Guevarra. But for "personal and health reasons," amid public appreciation his "good accomplishments" had cultivated through the years, leaving his post became a necessity. He right there and then emigrated to the US, with the sale of his house later in Subic making people think he would never set foot in it again.

2

Geography

As Zambales's southernmost town, Subic is geographically pinpointed on the map at 14.53 degrees latitude and 120.14 degrees longitude. It is bounded on the north by the town of Castillejos, eight kilometers away; on the east, the town of Floridablanca, Pampanga, is 73 miles away; on the southeast, 11-kilometers away is the city of Olongapo; on the west is the expansive South China Sea. It naturally sits nestled in between the Zambales Mountain Range and the Subic Bay, so it became known as, "The town where the mountains meet the sea!" It is quite accessible from the 139-kilometer-distant Manila by a car ride of only about 2.5 hours.

SALIENT FEATURES OTHER THAN THE FAMOUS SUBIC BAY

Origin of the Name Subic

How the town name "Subic" originated has three different legend-based stories to it. Whichever makes sense, however, is left wholly to readers' own study, based on pertinently compiled information. The first story is that the town used to be called "Hubek." This word is a "Zambal" derivative meaning "plow head." The word "Zambal" refers to the dialect of the indigenous inhabitants of the province of Zambales, and they are called "Zambale." Plowhead making was once a major home industry in Subic, and this is because of the place's abundance of "molave" (a hardwood species) in its forests in early times. But pronouncing "Hubek" was rather tongue twisting among Spanish explorers, so that they changed it to "Subic."

The second story is that the name "Subic" came from the Zambals' actual name for large ants that used to exist in great colonies in the locality. The Zambal tribe that first inhabited Subic had the peculiarity of using the letter "S" more often than the letter "H." The rest of the same tribe that lived in places other than Subic had retained use of the word "Hubek," rather than "Subic," in reference to the town's name.

Lastly, the third story pictures some Spaniards believed to be of the Augustinian Recollects, if not of other Orders, as those who had coined the name "Subic" themselves. When in the course of their exploration of Zambales in the 1600s they had asked a couple pounding rice by their home yard about the name of the place they had visited. Some piglets (called "biik" in Tagalog) happened to crowd around the couple's native basket, trying to feed on its rice content. Coincidentally, they just heard the couple shooing away the piglets by shouting "Shoo, biik!" at them. From that time on, the Spaniards left decidedly calling the place they had explored, "Subic."

Land Area

The town physically covers a land area of about 283.09 sq. km. or 28,309 hectares jurisdictionally divided among sixteen barangays, to wit (in alphabetical order): Aningway-Sacatihan, 777.10; Asinan-Poblacion, 403.00; Asinan Proper, 403.00; Baraca-Camachile, 70.2; Batiawan, 11,260.20; Calapacuan, 230.60; Calapandayan, 117.70; Cawag, 6,365.60; Ilwas, 15.00; Mangan-Vaca, 928.80; Matain, 42; Naugsol, 370.00; Pamatawan, 7,043.10; San Isidro, 181.4; Sto.Tomas, 82.70; and Wawandue, 18.60.

Ranked as the 7th biggest municipality in the province Zambales, Subic actually constitutes only about 7.5% of the province's entire territorial dimension.

Topography

A rolling, rugged mountainous terrain makes up about 76% of Subic's landmass, of which Mount Redondo, located southwest with an elevation of about 3,513 feet, is the highest. The next highest mountain range is Mount Balakibok located east of the town. It towers to 2,765 feet.

The Subic poblacion is a low, flat valley adjoining the Subic Bay and has an elevation of only about 0.7 feet. This used to see the area occasionally flooded for some short periods of time during either heavy rains or high tides, but a seawall and drainage works have proven effective control measures.

The inland areas are suitable for crop farming, as well as for wood tree and fruit tree farming. Had "kaingin" or slash-and-burn farming done by burning bush and potentially growing forests for the cultivation of upland rice been put under more effective control in the past, Subic's mountain ranges would have remained a lasting resource for lumber and other raw materials essential to profitable woodcrafts and rattan crafts.

In the town's coastal areas, on the other hand, fish farming thrives.

Soil Type

Mountain soils (undifferentiated) comprise around 14,063 hectares, and this area represents about 50.4% of the total land area of the municipality. About 6.1% or 1,700 hectares is of the Angeles Fine Sand classification.

Climate

Subic enjoys a generally pleasant maritime tropical climate. The months April through May are the hottest and December through February, the coldest—and require wearing of thick clothing, particularly at night. The wettest months last from July through October.

Temperature averages 80 degrees Fahrenheit or 26 degrees Celsius. Humidity, on the other hand, ranges from 75 to 80%. Two distinct seasons exist: dry and wet. The dry season is from March through June; the wet season, July through October.

The intervening months of November through February are neither too dry nor too wet. The wet season begins with as much as 10 to 20 inches of rain a day. Annual rainfall is approximated at 98.9 inches. Rains last for two or more successive weeks, and this duration is called "siyam-siyam" (or monsoon). Most storms or typhoons occur in August.

3

Pre-Colonized Civilization

Subic's pre-Spanish inhabitants were believed to be immigrants to the Philippines from a Malayan-Indonesian population stock of a primitive Negrito group, who remnants survived by living in remote mountain areas. They were called Negritos, Aetas, or Agtas. They were followed over the years by Malayan immigrants, who subsequently became the ancestors of most of the indigenous Zambales natives known as Zambals or Zambale. Where the Aetas average less than five feet tall and have black skin and kinky hair, the Zambals' progenitors stood more than five feet and had black, straight hair and brown complexion typified by almost any Filipino of generally Malayan physical looks today.

EARLY WAYS OF LIFE

Aetas' Domestic and Social Living Practices

The Aetas, aborigines of the Philippines, did not practice ordinary agriculture but lived mainly by hunting and gathering wild forest products. Their houses were built only as temporary shelters made of fallen branches and leaves. Their food consisted chiefly of rice and wild starch tubers. Food availability often determined the site of a settlement. Meat for their diet came mainly from wild deer and wild boar. They also engaged in catching monkeys, birds, wild cats, and large lizards for food. Butchered pythons supplied their most highly regarded meat diet. Insect larvae were a delicacy to them. Vegetables and fruits such as palm cores, bamboo shoots, edible ferns, mushrooms, fungi, rattan fruits and guavas also were part of their food. They were hunters by instinct, habit, and necessity.

Their most essential weapon was the bow and arrow. The bow was made of bamboo or palm wood with a rattan string, and the arrow was fashioned out of metal wire. They also used goods acquired from lowlanders in exchange for labor or forest-sourced goods. Most of them wore but scanty clothing that covered mainly their bottoms, and some went about entirely naked. They were generally superstitious and the basis of all their superstitions was the belief in the omnipresence of spirits ("anitos"), and all misfortunes, diseases, crop failures, and unsuccessful hunts were attributed to them. Some considered disease a punishment for wrongdoing. Serious diseases were believed brought by supreme "anitos;" minor ailments, lesser "anitos." They are admirable their inherent know-how of dealing with the challenges of jungle survival. With highly developed senses, Aetas' sense of direction and smell was extraordinary. They could track down a snake by its scent. They could tell the kind of meat a person had eaten. Their knowledge of their surroundings was amazing.

Beautifying themselves in their own way formed an inherent part of the Aetas' culture. They sharpened their teeth and marked their trunks and limbs with a knife or other pointed object. The marking or scarification process, called "ta-ad," was usually done at age fifteen or sixteen. The series of welts produced followed a regular pattern.

The wearing of necklaces was common among women. The necklaces were usually made of seeds (called "co-in-ta"), hard berries, buttons, or wood. Some necklaces were also made of fine woven strings of "bejuco" or hollow vegetable fiber and black crosswise strands (called "la-lo").

Aetas of both sexes wore bamboo combs as ornaments. In Southern Zambales, male Aetas wore leggings made of boar bristles ("Ayuban")—purportedly as a source of the power of endurance in long journeys.

In every marriage among Aetas, a groom always paid a price for an Aeta bride. The bride's parental consent was given to the marriage only if the groom was the highest bidder for the daughter he had chosen to marry.

Payment was usually in the form of tobacco, corn, knives, cloth, and forest products. Total value of payment was based on the girl's attractiveness, health, and strength. The girl's parents gave their consent if the gifts presented by the would-be groom were deemed sufficient. Prior to gift presentation, the Aeta suitor and his relatives first asked the girl's parents for her hand in marriage. It is only after a favorable response from them that the suitor and his relatives would come back later, bearing their gifts in exchange for the girl.

Songs and dances were the main forms of entertainment of the Aetas. They called a love song "dunuru." A kind of foot dance called "talipi" was popular among them, and it consisted of the making of a series of heel-and-toe movements performed to the tune of a native guitar or violin.

The Aetas' musical instruments were more highly developed than those of other primitive people. Their flute was made of reed, and the harp was improvised from a piece of bamboo. Their music was characterized by the constant repetition of four notes, the variety of which was now and then changed by changing the keys.

Childbirth among Aetas was highlighted with the giving of a name usually selected from names of trees, objects, animals, places, or a certain quality or deeds. The child might also have been given the name of a father, who then would have the word "pan" (meaning "elder") prefixed to his name.

If the child happened to be sickly or cried frequently, his name was changed. Aetas believed that if the child was sickly or fussy that the spirit inhabiting the place where the child was born was not pleased with the chosen name for him/her, hence the need for it to be changed; if the name was not changed then the child risked death.

Malayan Immigrants' Arrival

At the end of the Glacial Period, which historians refer to as the Pleistocene Epoch, seafarers from the Malay Peninsula of the Asian mainland sailed to, and established pockets of population in the Southeast Asian islands. The Malays were the first wave of immigrants to reach Zambales at the time when it was already a part of Luzon. Their arrivals drove the Negrito aborigines from the plains and valleys to the mountains. The Malays established themselves at the western coastal plains of Luzon between what is now Subic Bay and Lingayen Gulf. They saw a stretch of land that sloped down from the thickly forested mountain ranges in the east to the seashores in the west. They were later believed to be the ancestors of the early Zambals. Unlike the Aetas, who are distinguished by a small stature, black skin, kinky hair, and abnormally too long arms and legs in proportion to the body, the Malays exhibited medium height, brown skin, and regular body build.

4

Spanish Colonial Rule

The long history of Spanish colonization of parts of the world bears a distinct mark that makes it distinguished from the records of other European countries that vied with one another for their own pockets of power on the globe: Emphasis was laid on the spread of Christianity or the Roman Catholic religion itself. All expeditions sent to the newly discovered, promising islands throughout the Philippines were accompanied by missionaries, and this was by royal decree as a matter of policy. When Miguel Lopez de Legazpi established a settlement in Cebu in 1565, he was accompanied by an Augustinian missionary, Fray Andres de Urdaneta, who served as navigator but was responsible as well for establishing the pivotal position of the Catholic Church thereat, and this arrangement typified all other succeeding colonization that took place from then on.

Spread of Christianity

The Franciscans, Jesuits, Dominicans, and Recollects followed in succession after the Augustinians, in preaching all about Christianity in the

Philippines. Use of a sword and a cross was quite helpful for Christianizing work. Spanish soldiers indispensably helped the friars in laying the foundation of towns in chosen settlements, as well as in subduing and controlling their native subjects. Church baptism symbolized not only conversion into Christianity but also allegiance to Spanish authority.

The municipal hall called "Casa Real" served as a nerve center for Spanish endeavors to effect and conduct people's cohesion and submission. Of the two governing groups, the church authorities dominated the exertion of an almost all-encompassing influence in conditioning people's lives. Priests exercised temporal power and directed the selection of local officials.

The missionaries did much in imposing colonial rule. Their employment of force and preaching of a more attractive system of beliefs and doctrines weaned the attention of natives away from their ancient gods and goddesses.

Exploration of Zambales

Zambales was first explored in 1572 in the course of an expedition that covered the entire western coast of Luzon. Juan de Salcedo, the dashing grandson of Miguel Lopez de Legazpi, first Spanish settler in Cebu in 1565, led the exploration. When on a certain day Salcedo and his men were sailing along the coast of Bolinao, Pangasinan, which is located near the northern tip of Zambales, they happened to encounter a sampan holding captives out of a Zambal chieftain and his followers under the command of Chinese seafarer-warriors. For only conjecturable reasons, Salcedo and his men thought it wise to fight with the Chinese and free the native Zambals. As a result, the freed Zambals emerged from their captivity grateful, and thenceforth accepted and pledged allegiance to Spanish sovereignty.

But there were instances that saw strong native resistance to Salcedo and his group. In places where he ordered collection of tributes from the inhabitants as gifts for Spain's new ruler, King Philip II, the natives could only respond negatively—but only until ultimately forced to succumb to their masters. Their boloes, made up of thick-bladed lances with wooden handles and bows and arrows as their chief weapons, hardly matched the Spanish soldiers' own.

Founding of Subic Bay's First Shipyard

Although Subic Bay was found in 1572 by Salcedo to be ideal for establishing a naval port, his exploration findings only remained a mere report on paper for 313 years before action was taken on his recommendation in 1885. It was Cavite, adjacently facing Manila Bay, that was chosen, instead, as site of the main Spanish naval base in the Philippines. The Spanish Cavite Shipyard, which was built on September 1776, thus became the center of naval operations that included the building of galleons that plied the Pacific Ocean for international trade chiefly involving Mexico and Manila for years.

The Cavite Shipyard later proved problematic because of shallow water, unhealthy living conditions that gave rise to malaria and other diseases, lack of shelter, and difficult manageability in times of bad weather or war. Therefore, a military expedition to Subic was launched in 1868. Its findings duplicated in substance what Salcedo had earlier reported long in the past: Olongapo, then a budding Subic barrio, where natives used bancas for fishing and bows and arrows for hunting wild pigs, birds, etc. in its thick jungles, showed the most promising prospects for a military naval base, compared with Cavite, which is within the outskirts of Manila Bay. This hardly sounded like a wise choice in Manila, though. The vision of a rural assignment in an isolated, jungle-obtruded Olongapo area was a far cry from the city's titillating bright lights and other related urban sights. So, it took an issuance in 1884 of a royal decree declaring Subic Bay a naval port, and the Spanish Naval Commission's order in March 8, 1885, to construct in Subic Bay an "Arsenal at Olongapo."

After Salcedo's exploration campaign in Western Luzon in 1572, additional numbers of Discalced Augustinian or Recollect missionaries arrived and helped with the process of organizing the province of Zambales. As a new province, it included areas of coastal plains and mountain ranges from Subic to Bolinao along the Lingayen Gulf of Pangasinan. Zambales was named after its inhabitants, the Zambals. The villages that existed before the Spaniards' arrival became new towns: Subic, 1607; Masinloc, 1611; and Sta. Cruz, 1612. Thus, Zambales was one of the first provinces created by the Spaniards.

Founding of the Town of Subic

Discalced Augustinian Friar, Reverend Father Rodrigo de San Miguel, founded the town of Subic in 1607. In his own book, *Provincia de San Nicholas de Tolentino de Augustinos Descalzo*, his description of Subic, its people, and environment was as follows (translated from Spanish):
This town, whose church is dedicated to the Apostle Saint James, was founded

in 1607. It is situated towards the west of the island and the bottom of a beautiful cove. The conversion of this town came about after the preaching of Father Rodrigo on the falsity of its inhabitants' divinities. They used to adore the demons in the forests, and when once the minister of the true God was passing through, he saw a tree full of the seasonal, yellow fruit called mango. His inquiry from some natives he saw at the place elicited a reply that anyone engaging in the profaneness of cutting a branch or picking a fruit off the tree could surely suffer sudden death. On hearing this, he gave them a sermon out of fervor and zeal in the glory of God, to correct their deceptive belief. Taking a crucifix and saying the prayer 'Ecce Lignua Crucis,' he destroyed the branch of the tree and ate a fruit of it in the presence of the natives who, upon seeing that the priest suffered no harm thereafter, just believed in his teachings and they henceforth became children of the Catholic Church.

The book also contained the following descriptions of Subic: "Climate is healthful, and its products are rice and farinaceous plants. There is an abundance of drinking water, which flows in their vicinity East to West of two rivers called Baliti and Wawandui. In its forests are found different classes of wood (lumber), which is known in other points of the islands."

Parish Organization for Town Development

The Recollects greatly helped in organizing parishes, which later became pueblos (towns) with direct help of the Spanish government. The Negritos were included in all endeavors in this regard to make them subjects of Spain. A Spanish royal decree was promulgated on June 12, 1846, directing alcaldes, the military force, and provincial governors to encourage Negritos to assemble in villages so that they could be given lands to cultivate.

On January 14, 1881, another decree was issued providing for the following benefits to Negritos in exchange for their voluntary submission: 1) Protected life in pueblos; 2) Unity of families; 3) Concession for good lands and better methods of cultivation, including clothing for a year's duration; 4) Respect for their customs, and freedom to decide on whether or not to convert to Christianity; 5) Facilitation of their crop sale; 6) Exemption from contributions and tributes for ten years; and 7) Right to elect their local officials.

Under the town-settlement program, which was known as reduccion and patterned after the successful Mexican and Peruvian town-settlement schemes, people residing in scattered places were uprooted and forced to resettle in compact villages until the population reached 2,400 to 5,000.

Aetas' Predatory Raids

Although the reduccion created living conditions that were relatively more beneficial in most respects than what the Negritos had been satisfying themselves with for years prior to the Spanish missionaries' arrival in Subic, resettlement authorities' harshness made the natives feel oppressed. As a result, the maltreated Aetas could only resort to finding refuge in the mountains and conducting predatory raids on established settlements—obviously for retaliation and ready access to coveted life-sustaining provisions.

One raid conducted by the Aetas took place on May 1892, with Don Manuel Yparraguirre, Infantry Captain, reporting about it in his letter to the Governor of Zambales, who concomitantly held the rank and title of Captain General under the name Mariano Ricafort. (Appendix H shows the letter's details.)

Sufferings from Typhoons

On May 18, 1850, the Alcalde Mayor (equivalent to governor) of Zambales, Jose Sanchez Geurrero, reported to the Spanish governor-general of the Philippines at the time on the extent of damage that a typhoon that passed by the country on May 5, 1850, had caused in Subic. Appendix I details his letter-report.

Mayoral Disputes and Resolution

On August 22, 1897, the mayor of Castillejos wrote the mayor of Subic a letter regarding a questionable setting of mojons (cement landmarks) on the boundaries of the two towns:

The Governadorcillo of Castillejos, to the Govenadorcillo of Subic: As a matter of urgency relating to a letter of the Senior Inspector of the roads, I hope you would have the pleasure of returning to me, authorized or not, the certificate of land marking of both jurisdictions of this and that town, done by said official, because they demand it urgently from me and in case it is not authorized, please return it to me, explaining the causes, so that I can explain it in my part to the said gentleman who demands it from me, since it was already for days that I have sent it to you. And by doing so, I will feel obligated to reciprocate accordingly.

I wish God grant you more years,
Castillejos, August 22, 1897"

In reply, the mayor of Subic wrote back:

The Governadorcillo of Subic, to the Governadorcillo of Castillejos: In answer to your letter dated today, I would like to make it known to you that the principal citizens of this town refuse to sign the minutes of the land markings for the jurisdiction of that town and my town as that you had taken upon yourself to send me in triplicate, and their reasons for refusing are the following:
First: The cited measure did not state any agreement supposedly taken up when the Honorable Civil Governor of this province was present that the principal citizens of this town would cede to them the merited duty, like jurisdiction of that town from the big hill up to the site of Laoac, Aningway with the enclave lands of the same principal sites of that town, or the repair of all destroyed highways which exist in the transit from the site hill Pamataoan within six months.
Second: It is because the old jurisdiction of that town, which has been set forth in the alluded measure, is the big hill but not the Pamataoan River—a fact which is known to this town's principal citizens, as well as to Pamataoan's present and past elder citizens. However, if in your tribunal there is a boundary that suits your expediency, in the archives of my responsibility, such document does not exist, to convince said gentlemen.

I wish God grant you more years,
Subic, August 22, 1897
PLACIDO DELA PAZ

Beginning of the End of Spanish Rule

When Andres Bonifacio, a self-educated man of humble origins from Tondo, Manila, but turned Supremo (commander) of the Katipunan that he founded as a secret society sworn to win independence from Spain, proclaimed the Filipinos' open revolt against Spanish rule on August 29, 1896, a group of Katipuneros from Bulacan and Orani came to Subic and esatablished their headquarters and command post there. For Bataan and Zambales, the Katipuneros' Supremo was Mariano Medina, and with him as Subic's initial Katipuneros were Hialrio Logun, Gaudencio Mendigorin, Esteban Mendigorin, and Isidro Laanan. They were the first to revolt against Spanish forces, called Casadores, at Naugsol, a farm area of Subic. Led by Hilario Logun, they suffered no casualties in their battling action.

In the same year, the Katipuneros covertly assaulted the Spanish headquarters atop the Palibunin Mountain. This happened at two o'clock in the afternoon. In effect, the Katipuneros' revolt amounted to more than just the presentiment among the Spanish rulers that their days in power were numbered. Not long after the Katipuneros' Palibunin Mountain attack, another was planned against the main Spanish forces right in Subic town proper itself. As they reached and prepared to deploy at Calapacuan, which is about three kilometers away from the poblacion, they realized that that they could be outnumbered by Spanish soldiers and civil guards, so they decided to forego their assault plan.

Hilario Logun led another attack in Lata, a sitio within Subic's jurisdiction. Then when Spaniards, comprising one high official, fifty Casadores, and a guide were on their way to Olongapo, Katipuneros Gaudencio Mendigorin, Rafael Maliksi, Francisco Santiago, and forty other Katipuneros went to Cawag and there attacked the Olongapo-bound Spaniards while in the process of boarding a boat. In the aftermath, a few Casadores were able to escape along with the lone high Spanish official and his guide. But a great number of Casadores were killed, and they were all buried right in Cawag. Three Casadores were held captive, one Katipunero was wounded, and another Katipunero, named Maximo Mina, was killed. By order of Gaudencio Mendigorin, the dead Katipunero's corpse was interred in the Subic cemetery.

American Role in Ending the Spanish Regime

Without American intervention and help, Spain's rule in Subic or anywhere in the Philippines would have not come about as the Katipuneros had wanted and sacrificed their lives for. Significantly adding weight to this is the fact that where the Spanish Subic Bay arsenal at Olongapo was supposed to serve as a reliable defensive bastion of its naval might, poor planning and loose preparations rendered the port's overall strategic value to be anything but useful. Military planners' recommendations on the placement of four six-inch guns had not yet been carried out, and only four mines out of 15 were placed in its sea vicinities. There was no assurance they would even work. In short, the arsenal was hardly fortified to expectations. As a result, the Spanish naval fleet in Manila Bay was suffering from low morale when war broke out between Spain and the U.S. in 1998, following Cubans' own revolution against Spanish rule that jeopardized American business establishments in Spain's Cuban colony. Commodore George Dewey, Commander of the U.S. Asiatic Fleet, was then informed on April 25, 1898, that a state of war between America and Spain had come about, and he was ordered to attack the Spanish fleet in Manila Bay.

The Spanish antiquated fleet, which formed part of Spain's Navy that sustained its global empire in the sixteenth century, happened to be made up of only eight ships. These included ships with wooden hulls and the *Reina Christina*, flagship of Rear Admiral Don Patricio Montojo y Pasaron, the Fleet Commander. It had just arrived back at Manila Bay from its aborted stay in the Olongapo arsenal at Subic Bay (because of the port's logistical inadequacies). On May 1, 1898, it was sighted by Commodore Dewey's forces and thence attacked—with results reported thus: 167 Spanish killed and 214 wounded, and on the side of the attacking American fleet, none killed and some wounded.

As Montojo's Spanish fleet got totally routed, the Spaniards in Subic abandoned the Olongapo naval arsenal and took refuge in Grande Islands, located at the western entrance to Subic Bay from the wide expanse of China Sea. All in all, 1,300 of them—soldiers, friars, and civilians—were to later become prisoners who were known to have never experienced the same indignities as were suffered by their former subjects.

Near-Strife between American and German Forces in Subic Bay

Some two months after Admiral Montojo's loss of his entire fleet in his defeat by Admiral Dewey on July 5, 1898, the Filipino crew of the Spanish tobacco cargo ship, Compania de Filipinas, mutinied as Katipuneros and killed its Spanish officers. The ship had just then left Aparri, a town at the tip of Northern Luzon. Led by a Cuban-Spaniard named Vicente Catalan, the Katipuneros put up boiler pieces to appear to be artillery, hoisted a Philippine flag, and sailed for Subic Bay to help fight the Spanish forces there.

But as they demanded surrender of the Spanish garrison, a German ship, the cruiser, *Irene*, suddenly emerged in the bay from somewhere, with its commander ordering the Katipuneros to lower their flag and replace it with a white flag.

Being outgunned, Catalan saw his situation untenable, so he had no other choice but to opt for his ship's immediate departure. Commodore Dewey got word of this, and he ordered both the USS *Raleigh* and the USS *Concord* to sail for Subic Bay. As the two ships reached Grande Island, the German cruiser, *Irene* had no other choice also but to withdraw, with her anchor being inadvertently disconnected and left behind at the bottom of sea in her haste.

The Spanish garrison at Grande Island surrendered to the USS *Raleigh's* Captain Joseph Coghlan, who in turn, by order of Commodore Dewey, turned over the Spanish prisoners to Katipunero Catalan. Of them all, fifty-two, including friars, opted to remain in Subic, with all of the rest marched inland towards Castillejos.

Rift among Katipuneros, and Andres Bonifacio's Execution

At the time, the Katipuneros or insurrectos were no longer under the command of Andres Bonifacio, however. Poor leadership and disunity divided them into two factions, with the majority ultimately falling under the overall command of Emilio Aguinaldo, a twenty-seven-year-old mayor of the town of Cavite, who had succeeded in vanquishing troops of the Civil Guard and the regular colonial force in the province of Cavite, which became the center of insurrection. With the friars' inglorious order of Jose Rizal's execution at Luneta on December 30, 1896, on fabricated charges of seditious Katipunan connections, the rebels found themselves with renewed will to fight the Spaniards. But better arms on the Spaniards' side prevented them from winning. Then in a convention at the Katipunan headquarters at Tejeros, Cavite, delegates elected Aguinaldo president and relegated Bonifacio to the post of interior director. The latter did not cooperate; instead, he formed his own government.

In a fight that later ensued between Aguinaldo's and Bonifacio's troops,

Bonifacio got arrested. Found guilty after trial, Bonifacio was ordered by Aguinaldo to be executed on May 10, 1897. But even Aguinaldo himself and his fellow Katipuneros enjoyed no chance in winning against their better-armed Spanish enemies on the battlefield. So, they could only resort to guerrilla warfare, which the Spanish found doubly difficult to contain. Thus on December 1897, an armistice was negotiated between Aguinaldo and Fermin Juadenes, the new Spanish governor seated in Manila. In an agreement between them, Aguinaldo and his government would go to exile and get paid $800,000.00 by the governor. Hong Kong was Aguinaldo's chosen domicile in exile.

Town's Administrative Set-Up

Under Spanish rule, the highest position entrusted to Filipinos in any given town went by the title gobernadorcillo (little governor). The position was made to function with the assistance of other officials called teniente mayor, juez de policia, juz de sementeras, and juez de ganados. The old datus remained in a status quo but were given the title, "Cabeza de Barangay," now called "counselors."

Subiquenians who had served in the position of gobernadorcillo and Cabeza de Barangay during the Spanish regime are listed (alphabetically) below by category:

Governadorcillo	Cabeza de Barangay
Valentin Afable	Nicanor Afable
Natalie Balintos	Cleto Custodio
Francisco Custodio	Placido dela Paz
Placido dela Paz	Isaac Juico
Gregorio Juico	Herminildo Labaing
Basilio Mendigorin	Juan Macedo
Clemente Mendigorin	Norberto Mendigorin
Feliciano Mendigorin	Salustino Ponco
Francisco Mendigorin	
Macario Mendigorin	
Pablo Mendigorin	
Cornelio Perea	
Roman Ponco	

Segundo Reyes
Juan Salang

During the Spanish rule, a person's popularity in Subic had much to do with the nature and magnitude of his or her business or occupation. Understandably, those appointed by friars and other ruling authorities to occupy higher-level positions in the local government remained in enduring prominence.

Among Subicquenian natives, the most popular included (in alphabetical order) the Floreses, Laags, Laanos, Laaos, Labagaos, Labampas, Laborces, Labudiongs, Labuntins, Laconsays, and Mendigorins.

When America took over Spain's rule of the Philippines, civil government was established. From then on until the Commonwealth of the Philippines as a government set up got underway under the aegis of U.S. tutelage in all the fundamental aspects of democracy, the town head was called "presidente municipal."

5

American Regime

Spanish rule of more than three centuries left the Philippines a legacy of Christianity, one of man's greatest religions. An American take-over of less than half a century, on the other hand, left the country a legacy of the blessings of democracy-rooted education—a conceptual molder of life's value to mankind. That education is vital to human life is an undeniable fact known to most people. As is also universally seen, life is God-given but education is not, hence the self-manifested need for one to acquire it to carry on with life assured of a worthy future: enhanced usefulness to self, family, and society—and even to all humanity. As most people are also likely to agree, anyone can go on with life uneducated, but this is like one possessing an irreplaceable gift, yet lacking knowledge of how best to use it for all its worth. Quite palpably, it is for this reason that—as a matter of policy—education was a major concern that the U.S. had given particular attention to in its colonial rule in the Philippines. American tutelage on the fundamentals of the Philippines' present-day educational, judicial, civil service, military, and other governmental operations systems resulting in granting the Philippines its inveterately longed-for independence in July 4, 1946.

ONSET OF U.S. EMERGENCE

Earlier Period

Even before the Katipuneros' revolt against Spanish rule in 1896, different foreigners other than Chinese had long put up business establishments in Manila under the ownership of Americans, Englishmen, Frenchmen, Germans, and Japanese. Of thirteen foreign trading firms, seven were British, two were Americans, and one was German. This simply gives the forethought of just a few of these foreign nationals' being on Philippine soil at the time.

But within a year after Emilio Aguinaldo went into exile following negotiation and $800,000.00-payment by the time's Spanish reigning Governor Jaudenes, Manila suddenly turned into a focus of international rivalry involving Japan and other major European powers. The scene of a power vacuum created in Admiral Montojo's defeat by Commodore Dewey in the Battle of Manila Bay in 1898 sucked in a menacing influx of warships from Britain, Germany, Japan, and France. In another sense, Manila Bay abruptly became filled with warships of different countries because the revolutionary turmoil between ruling Spain and the Filipino Katipuneros led into anticipations of the rise of opportunities that could be taken advantage of for each foreign power's colonial ends.

It was a problem of Spain's own making that her colonized subjects learned to revolt against her, and Admiral Dewey was present in Manila only because of U.S. involvement with Spain's other major colony, Cuba. The Cubans openly revolted against Spain in February 1895, jeopardizing American business interests in their Spanish-ruled country. Brutalities of Spanish reign ignited Cuban insurrection to the endangerment of legitimate American interests, thereby warranting declaration of war by the U.S. against Spain on April 25, 1898, as a result of which, Commodore Dewey was ordered to destroy the Spanish fleet in Manila Bay.

Aguinaldo's Resumption of Command of Rebellion

When the Cuban crises kindled war between the U.S. and Spain, Aguinaldo decided to end his Hong Kong exile and come back to Manila. At Dewey's advice, Aguinaldo thought it wise to reassume command of all Filipino rebels against Spain, acting as a partner, if not an ally, of the U.S. His motivation was his inveterate hankering for immediate Philippine independence, but the time's realities rendered it unlikely, yet possible. The time's immediate need under Dewey's plan was Spain's surrender, with the capture of Manila at the least cost in terms of human lives. It was accomplished even without the insurgent Filipinos' assistance.

For Spain's Governor Jaudenes, on the other hand, Aguinaldo's unexpected return from his Hong Kong exile, in violation of their earlier $800,000.00-based agreement, appeared obviously to be anything but settling. He realized that his country was at a disadvantage, what with the menace of many nations' warships' present in Manila Bay, Dewey having captured his fleet, and the Spaniards fearing that they would be massacred by a vengeance-unified throng of Filipino rebels. Governor Jaudenes urgently needed to contrive an honor-saving way out of an unsettling war dilemma.

Staging of Mock Battle

With British and Belgian diplomatic intermediaries' assistance, Governor Jaudenes arranged with U.S. military commanders a secret agreement whereby a mock battle in Manila was to be staged—essentially to save lives and concomitantly spare Spain of the shame of surrender without a fight. Of necessity, it entailed U. S. forces' entry into the city without bombardment, just a token gun-fire exchange between American and Spanish forces, non-participation by Filipino rebel forces, and a pre-arranged Spanish signal of surrender that was to effect automatic ceasefire on both fighting sides. It was conducted on August 13, 1898, and that afternoon, for the first time, the U.S. flag began the flapping atop Intramuros, the old walled city that cradled Jose Rizal's martyrdom as a seat of Spanish world power for centuries.

When Aguinaldo and his own forces did somehow arrive at Manila on the eve of the pre-planned battle to attack strategically positioned Spanish forces, U.S. command told him bluntly he could not participate and would be fired upon if he decided to the contrary. Denied what could have been a proud entry into their own capital city, Aguinaldo and his men could only wax infuriated with the time's pragmatically dictated wait-and-see approach after a duration of more than two years of soured relations with their alternate nemesis in their attempts to gain independence.

Aguinaldo's Ephemeral Self-Ruled Republic

The mock battle in Manila between Spanish and U.S. forces was rather a knotty irony in the sense that where Filipinos and Americans were supposed to be allies in their fight with Spain, reality instead saw Americans and Spaniards as actual partners against Filipino insurgents. But this notwithstanding, Aguinaldo remained determined to set up an independent Philippine government. With the help of Apolinario Mabini, dubbed the "Sublime Paralytic" for his being the time's foremost Filipino political thinker despite a physical handicap, Aguilando, in his Cavite headquarters, promulgated Philippine independence on June 12, 1898, and promulgated at Malolos, Bulacan, a new government constitution on January 21, 1899. It had been approved by a Filipino revolutionary congress on November 29, 1898. Two days after promulgation of the Malolos constitution, Aguinaldo was installed as president of the first Philippine republic. He thence assiduously exerted efforts in organizing fundamental agencies and services—such as for schools, finances, military, and other aspects of normalized governmental functions, but all these proved short-lived and to no avail in achieving his vision of an immediate and lasting independent Philippine Republic. The Treaty of Paris, as signed on December 10, 1898, provided for bloodless transfer of Philippine rule from Spanish to American hands. The $20-million payment of the U.S. to Spain did not please the Filipinos, but to American historian Leon Wolff was ascribed the remark, in essence, that Spain accepted the money as a gift that had no connection to her handing over of the Philippines to the U.S., that questions of neither honor nor conquest were involved, and that the Filipinos' rebellion ended practically without charge.

Waging of Resistance War

In December 21, 1898, U.S. President William McKinley announced that the American stay in the Philippines was a policy of "benevolent assimilation"—with "...justice and right," not "arbitrary rule," to be in effect. When Aguinaldo learned this in a context devoid of references to "American sovereignty," he reacted by issuing a counter-proclamation condemning "violent and aggressive seizure" by the U.S., and so threatened war. His fight with the U.S. began in Manila with the killing of three Filipino soldiers' on the night of February 4, 1899, by two American privates on patrol. From then until Aguinaldo's capture at Palanan by Philippine scouts inducted into U.S. military service, on March 23, 1901, it was to ultimately end up with a total of 26,000 American soldiers committed to the conflict; some 4,200 U.S. and 16,000 Filipino soldiers (out of unknown nationwide guerrilla force) killed; and as many as 200,000 civilians fatally embroiled and victimized by the war's side-effects of unhandled famine and disease. All these caused Aguinaldo to believe that any further resistance was futile, and so he finally swore allegiance to the U.S. and then formally called on his compatriots to cease hostility. However, because of remaining recalcitrance among scattered die-hard rebels, hostilities did not cease until 1903.

Disunity on the War's Filipino Side

Petty rivalry-bred discord caused the rift between Aguinaldo and Bonifacio in their supposed common fight with Spaniards for Philippine independence. The nature of this instance sort of applied, too, in the case of General Antonio Luna and his associates in their fight with Americans in supposedly pursuing supposedly common ends. Although recognized as a most capable military leader entrusted with an overall command of the entire Filipino troops pitted against Americans, General Luna's intemperance and cruel tendencies aroused enmity among many of his peers. He was consequently murdered, and (unverified) rumors were that Aguinaldo ordered so. Disbanding of the Filipino regular army then ensued at Aguinaldo's directive in November 1899, and in its place were established decentralized guerilla commands in strategically located military zones. The rebels' almost unbridled ability to move around at will in population centers took a heavy toll in terms of civilian lives unfortunately sacrificed in battle cross-fire, losses that in present-day military parlance would be called "collateral damage."

SUBIC AS A WAR ZONE

Start of Hostilities

The core of Filipino military forces readied in Subic by Aguinaldo relative to the outbreak of the Filipino-American war on February 4, 1899, was posted mainly in the Spanish-built shipyard at Olongapo. Zambales was under the command of General Tomas Mascardo, who took also took charge of Bataan. A group of Filipino soldiers headed by a commandant of the

Philippine Marine Infantry, named Ruperto Arce, arrived in August 1899 at the shipyard to take charge of it, including the Spanish prisoners turned over months earlier to Katipunero Catalan. For any eventuality of American attack, fortifying preparations were made in the shipyard. Also, a gun battery was constructed at the Kalaklan Ridge, a part of a hill overlooking the shipyard, with use of one of the six-inch guns formerly in Spanish hands in the Grande Island.

Actually, though, Subic Bay and its former Spanish shipyard were hardly paid attention to as American and Filipino soldiers clashed elsewhere throughout the country. Since the showdown at Subic Bay between the German ship, *Irene*, and the Katipuneros led by Catalan, no Americans had appeared in it again. When it later occurred to the Americans, however, that into Subic Bay could be smuggled war supplies from Hong Kong for Filipino fighting forces' use, the bay started seeing regular patrols by U.S. gunboats. On one occasion, when the American lightly armed supply ship, *Zafiro*, entered the bay, it got suddenly fired upon by Admiral Motojo's formerly Spanish-owned guns manned—as if by a fateful role reversal—not by Spaniards this time but by Filipino insurgents. This incident marked the start of hostilities between American and Filipino forces in Subic.

U.S. Naval Assault at Subic Bay Shipyard

When the American ship *Zafiro* managed to stave off damage by Filipino gunners at the Subic Bay shipyard, it reported back at Dewey's Naval Headquarters in Cavite. The result was that the armored cruiser, USS *Charleston*, was dispatched to Subic Bay to silence the battery manned by Filipino gunners in the former Spanish shipyard. With her eight-inch guns, the cruiser quickly silenced the battery.

But no sooner had the ship finished maneuvering for return to Cavite when the Filipino gunners just suddenly took one parting shot at her—a show of defiance that only counted as a provocation of stronger responding action. Thus, to totally destroy the battery, the USS *Charleston*, USS *Concord*, USS *Monterey*, and *Zafiro* steamed across Subic Bay in September 23, 1899. The *Monterey's* huge 10- and 12-inch guns exhibited such a terrible onslaught that the Filipino gunners were able to fire back only once with their battery. When all the U.S. ships withdrew, the battery was totally put out of action, but the shipyard and the whole Subic town remained still in the hands of insurgent forces.

Capture of the Shipyard

The Subic Bay shipyard at Olongapo was captured in December 10, 1899, after an earlier province-wide launching of an insurgent-clearing U.S. Army operation led by Major Robert E.I. Spence. At 8:45 A.M., exactly a year after the signing of the Paris Treaty, the U.S. flag rose above the shipyard, with U.S. Marine Captain John T. Meyers in initial and temporary command with 100 Marines. On Christmas day, December 25, under the relieving and regular command of U.S. Marine Captain Herbert L. Draper, sailors and Marines discovered the gunboat, *Don Francisco*, believed to be the personal boat of President Emilio Aguinaldo, at the Binictican River near the shipyard. It was earlier reported to be loaded with some gold, purportedly for purchase of guns, but subsequent investigation uncovered no gold at all. Found with a sabotaged engine instead, the gunboat was repaired and brought to the shipyard.

Other War Encounters in Subic

At the most, ambush-instigated skirmishes were what constituted the nature of armed confrontations between American and Filipino fighting forces in Subic. Rebel guerrilla-conducted surprise attacks against the Americans took place on different occasions and in different places. Casualties on both fighting sides were generally light, as battle engagement mostly involved only light weapons—none of the kinds used in present-day warfare. Sites of ambuscades conducted by the Filipino Infantry included such familiar places as Mamirallik and Salungahin. American forces were also ambushed in Taquiling and Kayasan (in Subic) and Santa Rita (in Olongapo).

Outskirts of Shipyard as Places of Refuge and Peace

With the Olongapo shipyard placed under the control responsibility of the U.S. Marines, Subic and other towns in Zambales remained under the administrative and operational control of the U.S. Army. For Subiqueans not morally in accord with insurgents but desiring peace, Captain Draper offered Olongapo as a place of open refuge and peace in Subic and its neighboring towns.

With authority granted by the U.S. government, Captain Draper eventually managed to see the dawn of lessened insurgence in the town, and this came about via several pragmatic measures. First, he had an election held on January 28, 1900, with the aim of promoting the general welfare and securing the regular, routine, peaceful life of the people. Ballots cast saw election of Damaso Esteban as president, along with two others as vice president and secretary, respectively. Second, local government services were supplemented by U.S. Marines where appropriate—passing around food when harvest was poor, giving medical supplies as needed, and setting up of a school for the teaching of English. Third, a police force composed entirely of natives was organized. By mid-March 1900, more than 400 cedulas or personal tax certificates were signed by Captain Draper. Cedula-generated proceeds sustained cost of maintaining police services, sanitation, and road maintenance. Since then, the outskirts of the Subic Bay Naval Station, particularly Olongapo, a Subic barrio, gradually became urbanized through the years into a residential-business area markedly distinguished with nice dwellings and other edifices, well-paved streets, and clean surroundings.

FIRST PHASE OF U.S. RULE, 1898-1935

Appointed Commissions

U.S. President William McKinley had immediately appointed two commissions for the initial phase of American rule over the Philippines after Spain's rule. The first—appointed on January 20, 1899, with Dr. Jacob Schurman, president of Cornell University, as head—was the Schurman Commission. It worked to grant post-tutelage Philippine independence, immediate establishment of civilian authority with a bicameral legislature and autonomous provincial and municipal governments, and a system of free public schools.

The second was the Taft Commission, appointed on March 16, 1900. Headed by William Howard Taft, who later became the Philippines' 1st civilian governor, it worked for socio-economic development, education, and establishment of representative institutions as the three pillars of U.S. tutelage program. It established a judicial system, including the Philippine Supreme Court, replaced antiquated Spanish ordinances with a new legal code, organized a civil service system and the Philippine Constabulary, and defined the American colonial mission as simply for tutelage. Construction of railroads and highways, improvement of harbor facilities, expansion of markets for Philippine products, and encouragement of foreign investments conducive to national socio-economic development were also ambitiously attended to and carried out by the Taft Commission.

The Thomasite Teachers

The term "Thomasites" refers to all American teachers sent by the U.S. government to the Philippines starting in 1901 to establish a public school system, propagate basic education, and train Filipino teachers in the country. Their first batch of 500 arrived at the Philippines via the transport ship USS *Thomas* in August 21, 1901. On this account and because of the batch's being the largest contingent, the name, "Thomasites" became the designation of all American teachers who got involved in the education of the Filipinos—regardless of time or mode of their transport to the Philippines.

It was under Education Act No. 34 passed by the Taft Commission on January 21, 1901, establishing the Philippines' Department of Instruction that the Thomasites started the Filipinos public education system. This came about after the U.S. Army had to relinquish its side but inevitable responsibility of educating Filipinos within the domain of its operational control.

A few weeks before the 500 Thomasites arrived in the Philippines, 48 other American teachers arrived in the country via the U.S. transport ship *Sheridan*. About a year thereafter, another batch arrived, making the total 1,074 all in all as of 1902. An additional 1,000 more teachers were thereafter asked of Washington, D.C. by the Taft Commission.

Specifically, the Thomasites' legacy in concrete form since 1901 as pioneers in the national education of the Filipinos includes the establishment of the Philippine Normal School (1901), Philippine School of Arts and Trades (1901), Tarlac High School (1902), Quezon (Tayabas) High School (1902), and (reopened) Philippine Nautical School (previously founded by the Spanish Board of Commerce in 1834).

The significance of the sum total of their educational pioneering work is best reflected by the fact that the Philippines now constitutes the 3rd largest English-speaking country in the world—which in turn presently appears also, to account for the major presence of Filipinos in global employment.

Thomasites' Legacy in Subic

The (old) Subic Elementary School, which is now the Subic Central School, housing at the same time the Subic District Office, was an offshoot of the Thomasites' pioneering work in basic education for Subique ans, in particular. As in other Philippine towns that benefited from their services, students in grade levels 1 through 7 (until 1941) underwent schooling with a curriculum covering English, agriculture, reading, grammar, writing, geography, mathematics, general courses, trade courses, housekeeping, household arts (crocheting, sewing, and cooking), manual trading, mechanical drawing, free drawing, and athletics (baseball, basketball, track and field, tennis).

From the late 1930s until the outbreak of the Pacific War in 1941, the school faculty was headed by a principal named Mariano Bada, who later became a police chief of Olongapo City, with the rank of 1st lieutenant. The school faculty members known to have served with him were Ruperto Amian, Leonora Aranda, Purita J. Custodio, Villorita Gonzalez, Concepcion Lesaca, Eduardo Lesaca, Conrado Mercado, Liwayway D. Mercado, Borromeo Millora, Aurea C. Mojica, Adelaida Molina, Silverio Nepomuceno, Agaton U. Pagaduan, and Isabelo Soriano. Of them, Conrado Mercado later became a Schools Division Superintendent and Isabelo Soriano, Purita J. Custodio, Adelaida Molina, and Liwayway D. Mercado, all principals. Five of them later became U.S. Naval Base employees in Olongapo and in Guam, and the rest, retired teachers.

Although they did not all possess B.S. degrees, those without them attended summer school training that cumulatively earned credits for upgrading their professional qualifications and teaching proficiencies, with their hurdling of civil service eligibility tests later becoming their accreditation credentials.

During their time, "Speak only in English while in the school campus" was a rule religiously imposed upon and followed by students—on pain of confrontation in the principal's office if violated. Yearly, in assemblies in front of the school, were held inter-class inter-section contests in long-hand computations covering all four basic arithmetical operations: addition, subtraction, division, and multiplication—each in both single-column and analysis-requiring problem forms. Competitions of this sort, which simply required portable blackboards and participation by individual representative student contestants, were accompanied by other more elaborate (what with costumes required!) short literary-musical contests held with another participating school—actually the Castillejos Elementary School.

Primarily because of intensive (i.e., greater teaching input per unit course content), rather than extensive, classroom instruction (without sacrifice of course content coverage, of course), topnotch students finishing grade seven proved already qualified, in not few instances to teach. Even 4th-5th graders could already solve problems skillfully involving fractions, decimals, and their percentage equivalents, complex tasks whose results are more like results from high school students.

THE COMMONWEALTH PERIOD OF U.S. RULE, 1935-41

The Tydings-McDuffie Act

Actually a revised piece of legislation negotiated by Manuel Quezon himself when he went to Washington in March 1934, this act provided for a ten-year transition period to independence, during which the "Commonwealth of the Philippines" form of Filipino government would be established. It replaced the Hare-Hawes-Cutting Independence Bill passed first under a joint political campaign launched by Sergio Osmena and Manuel Roxas but opposed by Manuel Quezon on grounds of certain provisions disagreeable to him.

"I prefer a government run like hell by Filipinos to a government run like heaven by Americans," was a slogan then popularly attributed to Quezon at the height of his stature as a political leader aspiring to be president of an independent Philippines.

As a transition government to independence, the commonwealth aimed to have its own constitution, to be self-governing, with foreign policy staying a U.S. responsibility, and to have legislation on immigration, foreign trade, and currency system subject to the approval of the U.S. president. Despite certain particularly needed improvements in immigration and trade provisions of the act, the Philippines saw unencumbered its first commonwealth constitution framed in a constitutional convention that assembled in July 1934. Approved overwhelming by a plebiscite in May 1935, it established the political institutions incepted that year—and continued in usage as the constitution of the independent Philippine Republic effective July 1946.

The first election to the new Congress under the commonwealth was held in September 1935. Elected Philippine president and vice president were Manuel Quezon and Sergio Osmena, Sr., respectively.

General Living Conditions

Unlike elsewhere in the Philippines, particularly where landlord-tenant relationships and religious or ideological differences spawned social disturbances warranting the intervention of the Philippine Constabulary (the era's national police force), the great majority of Subiqueans lived quite peacefully throughout the commonwealth period—just as it generally did in the preceding years of the American regime. And this was cut short only with the onset of the Pacific War as a chain effect of World War II.

But in other parts of the country, rural revolts with messianic shadings sporadically flared throughout U.S. rule. In May 1927, some 10,000 followers of Florencio Entrencherado, a shopkeeper in Panay who ran in 1925 for the governorship of Iloilo on a promise of tax reduction, immediate independence, and control of Chinese and Japanese merchants, launched an abortive insurrection. As a colorum (false religion)-led revolt, it was misguided. Its leader claimed semi-divine attributes given by the "Holy Spirit and the spirits of Rizal and Father Burgos." In addition he proclaimed, "The hour will come when the poor will be ordered to kill all the rich."

Other Countryside Social Disorders of Divergent Causes

In Central Luzon, where tenancy as well as population density was highest, social unrest was particularly potent. The 1931 Tayug revolt in Pangasinan was colorum-connected. There were also other social movements with some religious or messianic overtones that later metamorphosed into secular or even revolutionary forms of existence or identity. Earlier, in 1925, the Association of the Worthy Kabola (Kapisanan Makabola Makasinag) had some 12,000 followers in Nueva Ecija under the leadership of Pedro Kabola, who called for liberation of the Philippines and promised aid from the Japanese. Another colorum organization called "Tangulang Kapatiran Malayang Mamamayan" (or "Association for an Offensive for our Future Freedom") was founded in 1931 with 40,000 followers of both urban and rural origins.

But the most important movement was the Sakdal Party. Founded in 1933 by Benigno Ramos, its political appeal was such that when it fielded its own candidates in the 1934 national elections on a platform of complete independence, land redistribution, and end to caciquism, it won some legislative and provincial slots. Because of poor harvests and disappointments with governmental inaction on peasant demands, its members, called Sakdalistas, numbering some 200,000, took up arms and seized public buildings in certain locations on May 2-3, 1935. It ended under control by the Philippine Constabulary only after about 100 deaths and Benigno Ramos's exile to Japan.

In 1938 the Socialista Party joined in a united front with the PKP (Partido Komunista ng Pilipinas). But their socio-economic goals were rendered almost untenable under the depression years—which summarily resulted in the collapse of prices and other profit-making aspects of business, thereby making them incite tenant strikes and confrontations with landlords and the Philippine Constabulary.

As a remedy, commonwealth President Quezon initiated his "Social Justice" program. It aimed to regulate rents but only achieved limited results, due to lack of funds to carry out the program, on one hand, and sabotaged implementation on the local levels as instigated by landlords and municipal officials, on the other. Thus, thousands of tenants found themselves evicted by landlords in 1939-1940, and this was particularly because of their insistence on receiving the larger shares provided for in the 1933 Rice Share Tenancy Act, but which was anathema to less scrupulous landlords.

Relatively Better Conditions in Subic—and Changes with the Times

Certain reasons account for relatively better conditions in Subic. The town had no extensive agricultural lands workable mainly by tenants. Farms were mostly homesteads in scope, and most families or households had more than one breadwinner.

In rural areas most farmers were self-supporting. Accessible mountains and forests served as sources of products needed to generate main or extra income, and unpolluted waters, aside from the Subic Bay itself, provided opportunities associated with marine-based industries—on a commercial scale or only for home use.

In urban areas, on the other hand, most families or households had their respective heads employed right in Subic (in municipal government and its instrumentalities), in the Olongapo shipyard, and in some other places like in San Antonio where Zambales's lone transportation company, Try-Tran, had offices. Other breadwinners were mostly self-employed and just carried on small-time businesses—tailoring, dress-making, refreshment parlors, salt-making, salted fish-making, butchering, sausage-making, market stall keeping, etc.

SUBIC

Self-sufficiency and simple living were what generally characterized Subic's actual socio-economic conditions for years before the Pacific War. During the era, a number of both American and Filipino retirees from military service chose to establish permanent residence in Subic, and this was primarily because of better times in the town—socially and economically. A most memorable American who lived in Subic, widely known for his great joy and gusto was a black popularly called Mr. Jim (Flippin). He frequented the clinic-pharmacy-residence of Dr. Albino and Mrs. Fabia Rodolfo, MD and pharmacist, respectively, as a friend fond of piano playing and singing along with his hosts' children. Other Americans included the Robertsons of Subic's Pamatawan barrio and the Rivers and Johnsons of Olongapo who temporarily relocated to Subic during the Japanese occupation.

At the time, the new Subic Public Market and its entire adjacent structures used to be what was yet a moderately wave-lapped expanse of a shore (called "aplaya") to which town folks would occasionally go at night or in the day to catch edible sea products—mollusks, crabs, fish, etc. A little distance farther out to the sea, all through the whole length of the Calapandayan barrio, was a portion of Subic Bay that used to be the site of "pukot" or commercial net fishing operations participated in periodically by up to 20-30 persons from different families—with each often receiving, for expended labor, a catch's fractional share often enough for a day's family meal.

One prosperous "pukot" operator in Subic was Pepe Del Carmen, who, as also a farmer in Agusuhin, was the nephew of a namesake, Pepe Del Carmen. He was the father of Dionisia Paulete, wife of Manuel Paulete, a past Subicquenian now domiciled in Hayward, California, as a retired USN sailor. Two others were the Ladao and the Evalobo families of the Subic barrios of Wawandue and Calapandayan, respectively. The Evalobo family happened to win first prize in the Philippine Charity Sweepstakes, and they had wisely invested a part of their sudden wealth in "pukot" fishing.

For small-scale net and "salakab" (hand trap) seafood gathering, the once-swampy area east of where the new Subic Municipal Hall now stands used to be a favorite site among not few families—particularly for home-use catching of fish, crabs, and frogs. Then, as a frequented place for catching fish (by dynamite or hook-and-line) and crabs (by "bintol" or baited-cage), not to mention oyster-gathering, right on the (old) Subic bridge, under which brackish water passes to and fro with the tides, proved useful for quite a while to many families. And what is more, the whole of Subic's surrounding mountains and forests even had made it possible, at certain times of the year, for meats of deer, pigs, bats, and various kinds of birds of the wild category to occasionally appear in the market, along with other more common kinds of food products.

Simple Though Dignified Living as Subic's General Way of Life

As Subic then had but a small number of families, and its natural resources more or less just matched the general populace's needs, the commonwealth period simply witnessed no unfavorable social disturbances of the sort that occurred in other places. What instead predominated in the minds of the general public at the time was that although the salary of municipal employees averaged only P60.00 a month (roughly equivalent to just $1.20 at today's P50.00: $1.00 rate), it at least sufficed most average families' day-to-day needs. In other words, the average income allowed people to live simply, but their needs were met. One full meal cost only about 5 centavos; a bottle of soda, 2 centavos. It is quite pertinent to mention at this juncture, however, that Subic at the time had yet to enjoy the blessings of modernity via the prevalent and assorted conveniences of today's living conditions in the town: electricity, multi-form transportation, air-conditioning, bottled and piped supply, computers, cell phones, and other kinds of work-simplifying and/or self-entertaining gadgetry.

However, in this time in Subic's past, hardly ever was heard the negative words heard now in media to characterize governmental or public life imperfections, words like "graft and corruption," "nangongotong," "racketeering," "scam" games, etc. Also, unlike after the onset of the post-independence era, when it seemed to be no longer so easy to trust anyone's words, be he or she a political leader, a government employee or official, or just a plain business person, it was simply the opposite in Subic in the commonwealth period. During that era, political leaders' pronouncements were firmly believed, and anyone in official uniform—military or civilian—was held in high respect and esteem. Male teachers reported for work in school in white coats with ties, commanding general respect, and female teachers went about highly respected as well. Policemen, just as their chiefs, commanded similar respect, with the general public simply looking up to them with great trust for general protection sans any show of apprehension. And where even the municipality's lowest clerk, a "scribinte," commanded high and healthy respect as well, the highest elected official, the mayor, was called "El Presidente" or the "President"—often with utmost dignifying obeisance because of practically non-existence as yet of money-rooted bureaucratic malpractices or politically disillusioning office malfeasances, which have later become collectively termed as "graft and corruption."

Listed below are Subic's elected municipal executives from 1900 to the present, categorized according to the period of their tenure and the title of their posts:

PERIOD OF TENURE	NAME	POSITION TITLE
1900-	Damaso Esteban	Presidente Municipal
1902-1904	Placido Dela Paz	Presidente Municipal
1905-1907	Salustiano Ponco	Presidente Municipal
1908-1910	Nicetas Lesaca	Presidente Municipal
1911-1913	Jorge Salang	Presidente Municipal
1914-1916	Jose Orosco, Sr.	Presidente Municipal
1917-1919	Juan Juico	Presidente Municipal
1920-1922	Esteban Felicitas	Presidente Municipal
1923-1931	Pedro Del Rosario	Presidente Municipal
	Alfredo De Perio, Sr.	Presidente Municipal
1932-1940	Numeriano Flores	Municipal Mayor
1941-1943	Cecilio Esteban	Municipal Mayor
1944-1947	Severino Salang	Municipal Mayor
	Alfredo De Perio, Jr.	Municipal Mayor
1947-1948	Leopoldo Lauzares	Municipal Mayor
1948-1951	Jose De Perio, Sr.	Municipal Mayor
1952-1955	Alfredo Afable	Municipal Mayor
1956-1959	Cecilio Panaligan	Municipal Mayor
1960-1986	Dangal Guevara	Municipal Mayor
1986-1987	Manuel M. Molina, Jr.	Officer-in-Charge, Mayor
1986-1987	Segundino Sandoval OIC,	Vice Mayor
1988-	Segundino Sandoval OIC,	Mayor
1988-1991	Manuel L. Molina, Jr.	Municipal Mayor
1991-1998	Manuel L. Molina, Jr.	Municipal Mayor
1998-2001	Leonardo Guevara	Municipal Mayor
2001-present	Jeffrey D. Khonghun	Municipal Mayor

Summarily, the commonwealth period—just as were the early years of post-Spanish rule until the mid-1950s from independence—was simply devoid of the likes of later-day widespread whining by Subic's general citizenry—as mainly traceable to the dark sides of politics. But the generally valued two-phased era was only later to see itself becoming just "gone with the wind," so to speak, and in exact paraphrase of the title of one of Art World's all-time great movie classics: *Gone with the Wind*.

The Creeping of War Tensions

Although most Subic folks believed particularly by December 1941 that war between the U.S. and Japan was approaching because of newspaper reports and earlier transparent war preparations as indicated by southward passages (towards Bataan) of horse-mounted and truck-loaded soldiers through the town, few expected that the Philippines would ever be conquered by the Japanese.

Months before the bombing of Pearl Harbor and right in Subic town itself, aside from Olongapo as a nearby site of the U.S. naval shipyard, security measures started to get stricter. At the Maquinaya checkpoint, posted U.S. Marines began meticulously inspecting passing vehicles. The checkpoint stood west of a roadside area within the U.S. naval reservation covering the entire mountain path or semi-zigzag road passing by the Olongapo shipyard proper, which was about 100 meters from across the Kalaklan Bridge.

When one evening a nine-passenger jitney with a couple of Subic families on the way to see a movie at Olongapo was slowing down for checkpoint routines, a woman inside said, rather unsurely, "Baka makapagkamaliang Hapon si Carling!" In English, this meant, "It may be that Carling gets misidentified to be Japanese!"

Actually, Carling was a young boy of 10 with a "sinkit" or narrow-slit eyes commonly characteristic of the Japanese. He then was one of the jitney passengers in the company of his (widowed) mother, who happened to be one of the daughters of a "Makapili" that later got incarcerated under collaboration charges. As each passenger was looked at the face by one of the U.S. Marines manning the checkpoint, however, Carling's eyes hardly mattered at all. The only adult male inside the fairly illuminated jitney was the driver, and the rest were two boys and four women. No questions whatsoever were asked.

Sudden Japanese Airplane Raids over Subic

"I was atop a coconut tree picking off nuts—for making cake—when I just suddenly heard whistling sounds, then loud explosions near me. When I went down with nervous curiosity, I saw machine gun fire hitting the beach and the sea yonder—and the 'punting' [Manila galleon-type sail ship] of the *Del Carmens* was burning, and there laid some bloodied bodies of people, hardly moving on the sand!" Thus runs a narration of Jose ("Joe") Gonzalez, a past Subique an resident of the Subic barrio of Calapandayan, who now lives as a retired USN sailor in Milpitas, California, about his eye-witness account of the Japanese bombing of Subic before noon of December 8, 1941.

Actually, Calapandayan was not the only site in Subic unexpectedly bombed by Japanese planes at the time. Just within the town proper only, three other sites were bombed: the frontage of the Subic Catholic Church, the Subic Elementary School, and the Ilwas Rice Kiskisan of Anicetas and Basilia Lesaca. The area hit in front of the church, which later showed a crater more than 10 feet wide and five feet deep, was the spot where an image of the Immaculate Mother was to later stand. The part of the school hit, on the other hand, was right at the middle—with damage not of such severity so that the building still stood, about 80% it its space usable, later.

But greatly regrettable casualties arose mainly in Calapandayan, as a result of which it remained a much-talked-about topic of news exchange among town folks even after the Pacific War. The ship that got bombed with an incendiary was owned by Jose ("Don Pepe") Del Carmen, who also ran in earlier years a cattle ranch in Iba and a farm cultivated to horticultural crops (dwarf makapuno coconut) and string beans in Agusuhin. Upon Subic's liberation by American GIs in 1945, Don Pepe's property in Agusuhin was used as a submarine base by the U.S. Navy. This was until some time after the Japanese surrender in September 2, 1945. "It was for this reason that my aunt, Dominga [Inggay] Del Carmen, daughter of Don Pepe," relates Josephina ("Pening") F. Bernal, spouse of a retired USN sailor, Dionisio Bernal of Hayward, California, "used to go to the U.S. Naval Base in Olongapo to collect rental payments on their Agusuhin property, on behalf and in the name of her mother, Flora Del Carmen, a half (Aeta) mestiza. Their property was used as a submarine base by the U.S. Navy in 1945."

Killed in the bombing of the ship was Peding Del Carmen, oldest son of Don Pepe. Other ship hands were just wounded. When U.S. liberation came in Subic four years later, Peding's brother, named Elyo, joined with the USN and never came back to Subic—not even once.

A particularly memorable side to this air-raid episode is that in the afternoon of the bombing when family members joined with their relatives who had already evacuated to nearby mountains, they had brought along fish of varying sizes that incidentally ended up as sea victims of the "punting's" bombing. They made a satisfying viand for dinner. The ship, when hit, was actually berthed and anchored near the Calapandayan beach, on a part of Subic Bay not far from Don Pepe's residence.

Evacuation of the Town

At the time Japanese planes air-raided Subic, most families had already left their homes in the morning to hide in the mountains. Bancas or boats with outriggers, and jitneys facilitated family evacuation movements, and one of the major evacuation sites chosen by families was a mountain called Galigao. Obviously, for the memory of a wartime evacuation episode, one Subic family thought it but proper that a son born in the mountain at the time be nicknamed "Galigo"—and he, in fact, is Eleuterio "Galigo" Morales, who is in his 60s today.

To Galigao flocked most families as a wartime evacuation center mainly because of its difficult-to-accesse location, as well as its convenient proximity to springs and river tributaries. Besides, it happened to have readily usable lumber for the construction of makeshift shelter. There was a sawmill in the mountain, and it was owned by Subic's Rodolfo family, who had graciously allowed free use of their lumber products by evacuees, in return for their commitment not to cut or deform such products in any way.

But evacuation proved not an easy task to most families, especially on the part of those with small children. Two families happened to be particularly lucky, however, in this regard. The burden of bringing along their bulky vital belongings—jars, chests, bags—to the mountain was well taken care of when a haul truck from the U.S. naval station in Olongapo, where bombing had also occurred, was expropriated by its own driver who happened to be the head of one of the two families involved. He was Ingracio Cruz, and he had obtained free use of the truck when the Olongapo shipyard owning it got evacuated too. As if by fate, the father of Galigo, Uden Morales, was a *kumpare* of Ingracio Cruz.

Among families who had better access to use of bancas, most evacuated to Cawag and from there later relocated somewhere else. As a hinterland barrio normally accessible only by a sea route within Subic Bay, Cawag is near Balaybay, another hinterland barrio that served as a springboard to other mountain-protected evacuation locales.

Families' Prayers During the Subic Air Raid

The power of prayer is believed by most people to be one reliable way of realizing a fervently hoped-for fate in life. Whether or not this is validly true in all respects is hardly possible to correctly make a valid conclusion about. But one particular relevant instance actually experienced by two families in hiding when Japanese planes raided Subic in December 8, 1941, is worth looking at. As about six planes flew right over Galigao before noon of that day from a northern direction, the two families fearfully entertained thoughts that the sun-exposed reflection of the Rodolfo sawmill's roof could be a bombing attraction. Thus, they could only pray, with their young children supplicating as well, with scared cries of "Diyos ko, iligtas mo po kami, Diyos ko, iligtas mo po kami, Diyos ko, iligtas mo po kami!"

For reasons open only to pure conjecture, all the airplanes did just pass by and disappear from up in the air, but, about four-to-five minutes later, the entire family group—and possibly all other evacuees in Galigao—just heard unnerving sounds of successive explosions emanating from the town, about six-to-seven kilometers away. And in the afternoon of that same day, the children and the families they belonged to learned from their elders that targets bombed in the town included the "punting" of Don Pepe Del Carmen, the Subic Elementary School, the yard of a kiskisan at Ilwas, and the Subic Caholic Church—which was not, however, hit at all like the other three targets.

Ransacking of Stores

Not long after the Subic airplane raid, news spread around that residents' emergency abandonment of the town ushered in what was expected: stores got robbed of most of their usable contents. Doors were forced open, with the biggest Subic store, owned by Pio and Ping, two Chinese partners, being the most ransacked. The store was known to house general merchandize but none of food category. It stood right where the L.C. Hardware and General Merchandise building is now located. Although as deeply aggrieved as the ransacking victims themselves, Pio and Ping, however, were to later wax fully cooperative with Subique an underground resistance that was to later get covertly organized against the town's conquering Japanese forces, who had quartered themselves in the old Afable mansion they commandeered for their garrison.

6

Japanese Rule

Imperial Japan ruled the Philippines for three years during the Pacific War. This was but a small fractional of time compared with the Spanish or the American reign over the country, but it proved particularly ignoble and oppressive, hence the most fearsomely loathed, it having wrought great suffering upon Filipinos. The Japanese rulers cruelly inflicted bodily harm on, and even outright beheaded, even only accused Filipinos as a routine means of governmental control. Unprecedented tyranny stripped a pathetically oppressed people of their once-enjoyed universal ways of freedom and self-sufficiency. Having earned Japan's attention even during the Spanish era, the Philippines since then up to the mid-1930s found itself gradually populated with 16,000 Japanese. This was only second to the Chinese, who aggregated over the years to about 100,000, but it cast an eye-catching shadow of a particularly marked difference: most P.I.-domiciled Japanese lived in Davao, chiefly engaged in a sapling nation's lucrative abaca industry—with the city they lived in dubbed by local boosters "Little Tokyo of the South." And quite unlike the Chinese, their home government embarked on an expansionist pursuit of a coveted future: Greater East Asia Co-Prosperity Sphere, encompassing spread-out air and naval bases to protect its conquests. Japan's aggression towards this end began with its invasion of China's provinces of Shanghai and Manchuria in 1931. For total rule over the Pacific, it treacherously attacked the U.S. Navy at Pearl Harbor on December 8, 1941. It sneaked into and attacked the Philippines, too, on the same day—with Subic itself, particularly the U.S. Naval Base at Olongapo, targeted, among other places. After the USAFFE-suffered debacles at Bataan and Corregidor in 1942, Subic, like many other Philippine towns, suffered socio-economically amid a traumatic, three-year quagmire of general inadequacy, health decline, restricted liberty, and home insecurity generated by Makapili-aided Kempetai surveillance. But thanks to General MacArthur's, "I shall return," promise behind his USAFFE's defeat, fulfillment of which saw him back again to Philippine soil with U.S. Liberation forces' landing at Leyte on October 20, 1944, Subic got freed at last of a life-dislocating scourge of Japanese rule. On January 29, 1945, V-sign waving American GIs were welcomed with overwhelming joy by euphoric Subiqueans. And that day was followed, seven months later, or on August 1945, by the emergence of the first weapon of mass destruction calculated to end all world wars, if not civilization itself. The world's first nuclear bomb all but obliterated Japan's industrial cities of Hiroshima and Nagasaki, ultimately humbling the nation into unconditional surrender at Gen MacArthur's terms, signed aboard the battleship Missouri on September 2, 1945, at Tokyo Bay. Tens of thousand got instantly or slowly killed by just two bombs—thanks to the work and influence of one of the greatest scientists of all time, Albert Einstein. He was wisely instrumental in President Franklin D. Roosevelt's decision towards the weapon's invention, which to this day has remained an assurance only of any two combatants' mutual annihilation once bilaterally used against each other.

OCCUPATION OF SUBIC

Pre-Invasion Operations

A hardly expected prelude to Japanese soldiers' march of conquest in Subic was the town's bombing by aircraft before noon of December 8 (Sunday), 1941, the very same day Pearl Harbor was attacked by carrier-launched airplanes. The raid over Pearl Harbor was launched at dawn; in the Philippines, it was some ten hours later, or actually before 12 o'clock P.M.

From a military standpoint, the Subic raid was inconsequential, except for the one carried out in its barrio Olongapo, site of the U.S. naval shipyard. In

Subic proper, there actually were no military installations whatsoever in existence, unlike in the Olongapo Naval Arsenal, as well as in Grande Island or Fort Wint, just about two miles across it, within Subic Bay. In both places, there were gun emplacements as defense fortifications, not to mention war boats at anchor or in patrol here and there. But why an invading Japanese command had to include the Subic Catholic Church, the Subic Elementary School, a rice kiskisan, and a galleon-type of (wooden) ship as bombing targets in Subic town—where non-combatants and only civilians were betrayed barbaric ruthlessness in all respects. And a supplemental proof in this regard was right the infamous Bataan Death March—an appalling war episode concretely reflecting man's devilish inhumanity to man—as witnessed by the thousands of merciless deaths that it exacted among weakened, sick, and wounded USAFFE soldiers sadistically forced to walk to an internment camp 67 miles away.

The rationale behind the Japanese's 1941 bombing of Subic town was not only to enjoy complete control over, but also exact absolute submissiveness of, their would-be subjects by fear instilled in their psyche. But it totally failed, in spite of the many human lives it exacted. It so intensified the ruled populace's hatred that it simply got nowhere in its supposed ultimate goal of winning solid allegiance of a whole people.

Evacuation of Town

Before conquering Japanese soldiers marched into Subic, most fear-struck folks had already fled their homes and evacuated to far, hilly outskirts and mountainous hinterlands that family heads saw ideal for a wartime refuge. The town began to be all but totally abandoned a few hours before it was bombed. News of the bombing of Pearl Harbor some hours earlier, learned from civilian workers at the Subic Bay U.S. Naval Base, had spread by radio and word of mouth. Many families had enough time to evacuate Evacuation snowballed from the time sounds of explosions were first heard from the direction of a 15-mile or so distant Bataan. There, General Douglas MacArthur's USAFFE forces battled indomitably but to no avail with determined Banzai-geared Japanese onslaughts. For one reason or another, only a few people remained in town, with all others fearfully fleeing their homes for refuge in the mountains. Then it later just suddenly became news by word of mouth among evacuees that some of those who remained in town were said to have ransacked its biggest store of the time: Pio's and Ping's

General Merchandize Store. Its contents of cigarettes, canned goods, carpentry tools, flashlights, leatherwear, etc. were all looted.

Evacuees' Way of Life in Hiding

Although new to the inconveniences of evacuation life in the mountains, families easily learned how to adjust, nonetheless. Shelter was exigently built as makeshift sheds out of readily available materials in abundance in the nearby forests. Water was tapped from wells dug only a foot or so deep when located near brooks or rivulets. General household needs, especially food, gave rise to a sort of a flea-market in a hinterland area called Panuliyan, which, as the only one of it kind, served as a bargain-and-barter center for the exchange and acquisition of goods, which largely comprised food items—rice, dried fish, fresh meat, salt, sugar, etc. The place was actually a part of a homestead owned by the Fajardos of Subic, whose head at the time was the municipality's incumbent Police Chief, Victorio M. Fajardo. Only their good nature accounted for their having allowed the use of their homestead free of any obligation to evacuees and market sellers and buyers alike.

Another family who graciously allowed free use of their property by evacuees, most of whom were their neighbors, was the Rodolfo family, headed by Dr. Albino Rodolfo, Sr., MD, whose wife was Fabia Rodolfo, a pharmacist. With three children, they had an only son, Albino Rodolfo, Jr. He saw action in Bataan but was fortunate enough later to successfully elude the Death March by escaping from Japanese captivity to join his parents in Galigao, the name of the mountain his family and their town neighbors had evacuated to. The Rodolfos happened to own a sawmill in Galigao, and they had allowed free use of their lumber products for evacuees' erection of temporary shelter, where cutting pieces needed for roofing or makeshift shed supports or floorings was acceptable.

As evacuation to the mountains fell on a dry season, it was propitiously made possible for families to live in shelters with roofs made only out of otherwise leak-prone materials—largely cogon and talahib, used roughly for roofing and walling purposes. Unexpectedly to some extent—hunger and disease, plus the dehumanizing atrocities of an invading cruel enemy were to cause them the gravest wartime hardships they ever experienced in life.

Soldiers' Pacification Campaign Among Civilians

Upon setting foot in Subic following the Fall of Corregidor in May 6, 1942, which followed the fall of Bataan a month earlier, or on April 9, the first thing Japanese soldiers did in Subic, which they found scarcely populated, was to look for and launch a pacification campaign among civilians. They then knew most families had already evacuated to the mountains. Actually, this advance move was taken by families largely because of fears bred by their knowledge of Japanese soldiers' brutalities on the hapless victims they conquered. Their much-feared atrocities included rape of women, the forced taking of people's personal effects (particularly watches), physically harming or even outright killing with guns (shooting in the head) or Samurai swords (beheading), and even the throwing of babies up in the air, only to bayonet them as they fell.

Just as important to their purpose the invading soldiers also won solid collaboration from pre-identified Makapilis. Known also as Ganaps or Sakdals, five of them were the most well known in town. Three of these were later incarcerated as collaborators. Two who were assassinated by guerrillas before American GIs liberated Subic in January 1945. As Subiqueinans' disliked impinging on peoples' sensibilities, such collaborators' could be only identified as Ganap 1st, Ganap 2nd, Ganap 3rd, etc.—with the words Ganap, Sakdal, and Makapili being synonyms in Tagalog for "maka-Hapon" (or "pro-Japanese"). The ranking order for them (1st is highest) is in accordance with the extent to which they showed their allegiance to the Japanese—which they practiced mainly by revealing identities of guerrillas or Subiqueinans who had joined with the Subic anti-Japanese underground resistance.

Soldiers' Visitation Trek to the Mountains

The scenario of Subic's being practically without a population to rule over made it necessary for a couple of platoons of Japanese soldiers—with Ganap 1st, the only Filipino, in their company—to go up to the mountains themselves and talk hiding evacuees into going back home. In their mountain trek, they paid attention first to more prominent families, understandably, to more effectively entice other families to follow suit without further ado—with the leading families' example of a back-to-town life serving, in the process, as sort of a lure.

For this, Galigao was the first and principal place visited, it being where the highest number of prominent families had gone to for hiding. To it and its vicinities had then evacuated the families of Dr. Albino Rodolfo, Sr., Jose Dela Paz, Sr., Subic Police Chief Victorio Fajardo, Ingracio Cruz and his bilas, Uden Morales—to name just a few.

When advance news of the visitation reached those in hiding, young ladies were advised by their elders to wear dirty clothes with some chicken or pig blood splattered on them—as sort of a psychological deterrent to potential rape or any other malicious advances that could be perpetrated by any ill-disciplined Japanese soldiers. It was then a notion of the time that Japanese men had an inherent predisposition to staying away from any women who appeared dirty, particularly with blood spots on them. It also became a popular belief spread by word-of-mouth among the general populace that perpetration of atrocious war crimes like rape and all other forms of physical harm to people was ordinarily practiced more by "Koryanos" or Koreans drafted into the Japanese Army, than by Japanese native soldiers themselves. Since 1910 when Japan had annexed Korea as a protectorate, all of its citizens were governed under the Japanese Empire.

Right into the Family Rodolfos' Galigao sawmill marched a company of the Japanese Army mid-morning in May 1942. Four other family groups had assembled with them, in anxious, fearful expectation of the conquering forces' arrival. But there was no way the hiding evacuees could tell as to which of the army visitors—all in virtually identical battle uniform—were native Japanese soldiers and which were Korean draftees. The soldiers simply looked alike in characteristics. Besides, they all happened to demonstrate good demeanor, especially their captain, who, distinguishable by his sidearm, Samurai sword, and insignias, spoke good English and acted in a gentlemanly way.

Their Ganap guide was quite familiar to the visited families. Obviously with great gusto, as if he was enjoying having power, when he had been a nonentity before, he was the first to address the assembled groups. He assured them that all those in hiding in the mountain could already safely go down back to town, and that there was no longer any cause for anyone to feel afraid or worry. Afterwards, the Japanese officer, who looked young, mild-mannered, and smiling, unexpectedly went out of his way to show a bottle of quinine and ask at the same time if there was anyone in the group affected with malaria—which happened to be actually one of the most rampant side effects of the war, along with dysentery and typhoid. It happened, though, that no one in the group had yet become sick, so Dr. Albino and Mrs. Fabia Rodolfo just thanked gently the visiting Japanese officer. When the soldiers left, almost everyone in the group could only heave deep sighs of relief, while "Aling Fabia"—as Mrs. Rodolfo was then popularly called—casually picked up the .45-caliber pistol she had sat on, atop a pile of lumber during the audience with the Japanese soldiers, and handed it over to Dr. Rodolfo.

Unexpected Post-Evacuation Hardships of Resumed Town Living

Hard back-to-town readjustment problems awaited families upon resettling their homes from their months-long perseverance of coping with the uneasy demands of emergency living in the mountains. Far different from Ganap1[st]'s assurances, which simply smacked of self-serving ingratiation with his chosen Japanese masters, the Subic families' return to town was to predestine themselves to three years of misfortune and misery, bitter hardships never before experienced in all their lives. In the mountains they had left as evacuees, the situation was generally like being with a group, socially carrying on a camping activity. But there was a great difference, and it rested mainly with the fact that while outdoor fun is basically the aim in camping, protecting or saving life was the counterpart aim in evacuating to the mountains.

Thus, as these evacuees were assured of enjoying once again a worry-free, normal community living upon being back in town, families affected just found themselves mired in a reverse situation. In place of having their normal lives restored, what instead was to fearfully stalk them for three years was a scourge of hunger, disease, stifled liberty, endless home insecurity, and other governmental impositions and restrictions anathema to sound family socio-economic structure and, therefore, to that of the whole country.

Grappling with Hunger

Hunger was the first hardship most families suffered upon settling back home from their mountain evacuation. But lack of money for buying food had little to do with it. Instead, it ensued as a direct result of the invading Japanese forces' plundering the captive country for whatever they envisioned had worth to them. The Japanese victors at Bataan and Corregidor schematically looted food storages and confiscated crops and livestock for their own use, not to mention for the Japanese in Japan.

Because of this and harbored fear, small independent farmers eventually engaged in "just enough" crop and animal production—or only to a level of self-consumption but with marginal surplus for income minimally needed to answer for their own other necessities. Thus, the wartime presence of the Japanese in Subic and in other Philippine towns veritably became, in itself, a severe drain to the very victuals of a once well-developing nation so ill-fated as to fall under the rule of what simply later turned out to be its worst colonizer ever.

Indeed, due to an enemy's seemingly morbid pursuit of conquest, what was once a generally peaceful, contended Subic became transformed into a languid, weakened town. Not long after evacuees' homecoming from their hiding places in the mountains, most of them would eventfully walk the streets hungry—with many poorly nourished and gauntly sick for some time. The scarcity of rice as a staple food, and of other products almost everywhere compelled many families to eat only two meals—at times even less, if at all, a day. In not few cases, even main meals or lunch and supper consisted only of thin lugaw or porridge—rice cooked with sweet potato tops and some dried fish—if it was available—watered down to create an illusion of nutrient quantity by sacrifice of quality.

This starvation-level common food intake was what circumstances for some time had forced upon even families of average status, so that eventually household members from parents to children just fell gravely sick, one after the other—and even simultaneously including both parents. Where families suffered instances like this, only the open-handedness of relatives elsewhere and more fortunate neighbors and friends around proved greatly instrumental as seemingly a God-willed oasis of last-resort source of help—materially and morally. But among those who happened to be helpless, life for them just went on dismally or simply ceased, as proving true Darwin's biological doctrine on survival of the fittest: "In natural selection, only the fittest or aptly adaptive among earth's living things enjoy inherent potential for perpetuation of their kind."

Hunger's Most Telling Negative Effect

The extent to which hunger went among Subiqueinans, including those living in its more urbanized Olongapo barrio during the early phases of Japanese rule, was such that food scavenging had become a common sight in the old Subic Public Market. As the only place where buy-and-sell business for commodities got transacted twice a week between consumers and merchants who mostly came from other places, its premises ordinarily got littered with trash made up partly of food wastes. The market's refuse was the only hope for the most seriously hungry at the time for any morsels deemed somehow to be still with a remnant nourishing value. As it was, even already chewed sugarcane pulp retrievable from anywhere would be picked up and re-chewed by the extremely starved, who moved about very listlessly on the streets in their rag-like clothes in extremely emaciated bodies. The result in the long run just sadly saw unlucky victims either getting seriously sick or dying unnecessarily.

Hunger weakened people, leaving them susceptible to diseases that would otherwise have not affected them. While the weak, the very young, and very old were natural victims to disease, at this time even those who would have been in the prime of their lives succumbed to diseases. Malaria, dysentery, and typhoid were the most prevalent edema-accompanied ailments that downed many evacuees not long after resettling their homes in town, and untimely deaths occurred almost daily—with corpses just wrapped in old mats and buried in the cemetery without a coffin or benefit of church-administered formalities.

The whole thing was such an unsettling scenario that one could only grimly expect continued decimation of Subic's populace, particularly where a void of strong natural immunity or resistance to disease or hunger compounded by dearth of medicines prevailed.

Instinct-Driven Struggle and Will to Survive

From a purely scientific standpoint, the unprecedented onset and rampancy of sudden poor health among evacuees shortly after their trek back home in town from their months-long hiding in the mountains was of bacterial and/or viral etiology. Cause directly came from malarial mosquitoes and pathogens carried in water, air, or even food that became contaminated in one way or another. Their exposure for some time to a jungle environment that was comparatively less protected from nature's harmful elements was virtually an invitation to risks of health impairment while hiding in the mountains. Among the affected who obviously were gifted with vigorous genes and, therefore, had stronger resistance to pathogens, medication by the use of herbs—necessary because of the dearth of pharmaceuticals at the time—proved effective. But among those who simply happened to have less resistance, inadequacy of both food and proven medicines was a sure, permanent goodbye to all! The problem aggravated the afflictions of many to a point where even the strongest natural defenses of those with a robust genealogical nature had a very difficult time.

Summation of the actual case in wartime Subic runs thus: food inadequacy as a predisposition to hunger concomitantly led to under-nourishment, which, in turn, caused lowered natural immunity or body resistance against an equally dangerous enemy of biological etiology. And then where medicines were supposed to come in handy for the already sick, these could hardly be obtained anywhere. This was because of hoarding particularly by the Japanese forces themselves, to meet their own need.

Coconut: Virtual Miracle Food Supplement During the Japanese Regime

For food when the staple crop, rice, was unavailable, various substitutes were relied upon—cassava, sweet potatoes, and corn, but only as supply became available. Ordinarily, the grated meat of coconut is commonly used only for cake making in most households in Subic and in most other places in the Philippines. But all through the war years it proved to be a high-carat gem of nourishment for most of those who got sick. It was mixed as ingredient (milk only or whole grated meat on case-to-case basis) with cereals, root crops, and particular kinds of leafy vegetables. Where grated meat was mixed with boiled corn kernels with little salt, the whole product was called "binatog;" if with boiled and ground root crop like cassava plus sugar, "tinupak." When unshelled, matured coconut meat is broiled, the resulting product is a tasty "castanyog," and this is known to have significantly helped save from hunger a great number of people in Manila, where food scarcity was most severe. Coincidentally, coconut also found apt use as cooking oil or lamp fuel, and it is generative of a cleaner and brighter flame than kerosene fuel, but it became suddenly just as scarce.

Another coconut product particularly valued at the time for its nourishing value was unfermented coconut toddy (not coconut water from inside the coconut fruit itself but juice extracted from coconut shoot), and toddy undergoing fermentation called "tuba" (actually a kind of coconut wine still under fermentation). Still another coconut-sourced food that helped nourish back to normal health family members recuperating from post-evacuation sickness was fresh "ubod"—a product sourced from coconut trunks. All the three coconut products just mentioned are known to be rich in carbohydrates, proteins, and minerals, not to mention fresh vitamins. Other kinds of fruit tree products upon which Subic folks depended upon for nourishment during the Pacific War included mango, santol, suha, duhat, balimbing, guava, etc., but coconut was the most treasured, chiefly because of not only its higher nutritive value but also continuous fruiting throughout the year.

Farming Barrios and Aetas as Oases of Relief for People's Hunger

If hunger in Subic found some alleviation at the time, small independent farmers in far-flung barrios and Aetas of the mountains in Zambales greatly accounted for it. From them were obtained by barter most of the supply of various food substitutes for rice—and even rice itself when plentifully available—that were urgently needed by many urban families who could not otherwise rely on other sources. During the early part of families' reorganization of their lives for post-evacuation readjustments they had to cope with, their travel to hinterland barrios and mountain sitios where food was not in shortage was simply an extreme necessity for emergency food procurement. This then became a practice for some time, as no regular market days could be held yet under the circumstances. Barrios in different towns of Zambales that became a wartime by-word for "no food shortage problem," to which urban folks flocked for food-scrounging purposes were Balaybay, Pamatawan, Kanaynayan, Amungan, Santa Fe, Wacon, Maloma, and Pundakit—to mention a few.

The "Dandani Naibos ti Tagapulot Tayo" Incident

In English, this phrase in Ilocano, a major Filipino dialect next to Tagalog, means "Our sugar got nearly all consumed!"—and it was about an incident that actually took place in Balaybay (once a Subic barrio that later became a barrio of Castillejos) during Subic's wartime hunger period. At that time, travelers from Subic and Olongapo needed to go to even far-flung places just to find and buy any kind of food for their families. One day a family in Balaybay, a barrio of mostly Ilocano farmer inhabitants, was busy processing their sugar cane, while many urban travelers had to wait until sugar was produced that they needed to buy. This native process entails using a "cabyawan" or crusher machine to crush the sugarcane stalks by carabao power, and boiling the extracted juice with use of a big pan called "cawa," and using the left-over cane pulp as fuel. Manufacture was done in open air, with only the stove roofed but without a wall.

As a common procedure, the impurities in cane juice come out with dark brown froths while the cane juice is boiling. The non-needed bubbles are scooped from the boiling juice with use of a screen ladle, with the collected foams just trashed or stored for hog-feed supplement.

For this reason—and by tradition, as well, kibitzers are allowed to participate, by group, in what is called in Ilocano as "lab-lab"—the practice of scooping boiling cane juice's froths out with use of cane pulp pieces as ladles—with the scooped foams not trashed, however, but sucked into the mouths of the participants—repeatedly until juice viscosity allows, or the signal for stopping the "lab-lab" is given.

Now, when a stop signal—in the incident—was given by the Balaybay sugar manufacturer's lips, it happened that the number of those who took part in the traditional "lab-lab" session were more than usual—actually some twenty urban travelers, a few barrio bystanders themselves not counted. As a result, the actual quantity of canned sugar (piece-by-piece form was done away with) produced fell short of what was expected—less than half of a can, instead of a usual produce of two or more cans—thereby making the manufacturer exclaim, "Our sugar got nearly all consumed!"

Actually though, what could have substantially accounted also for the incident's shortfall in the manufacturer's expected sugar output was the fact that the twenty or so urban travelers had offered to buy "gina-ok" or molasses-rich sugar syrup. It was scooped out of the already sticky boiling cane juice—i.e., before turning into solid sugar, and poured into boho containers prepared in advance. Because of the widespread problems of food shortage, each traveler bought two to three tubes, paying cash or in kind (jewelry and clothing).

An Olongapo Family's Unforgettable Debt of Gratitude to Aetas

"I was still young at the time, but well remember how really helpful to my family the Aetas were, for they profusely supplied us with food substitutes for rice—corn and sweet potatoes in particular, and we simply could never forget that without them we might have not lived to this day!"

These are the very words of Reuel Bundang, SRF retiree of the Subic Bay U.S. Naval Base who is currently connected as a naturalized U.S. citizen with a private security firm in California. Reuel says that he bartered dresses and shirts hand-made with a sewing machine by his mother with the use of thread loosened from socks. The Aetas his family had befriended were simply all so kind that they concerned themselves with whatever reliable, particular kinds of food substitutes for rice to bring to his family.

"The variety of sweet potato they regularly supplied us with," says Reuel, "had such degree of sweetness that even the water in which it was boiled was tasty and seemingly nutritiously sweet enough to drink like coffee."

"Because of their goodness," continued Reuel, my father had made it a point after the U.S. Liberation to go back once in a while to Amungan, the Iba barrio we evacuated to, just to renew friendship with and present to them personal gifts."

The Day of the Arbularyo

"Albularyo" or "herbularyo" is the Tagalog word for a folk-medicine doctor. As so many people got sick in wartime Subic, "herburlayos" became particularly relied upon for cure. To some extent, this was because of the sudden scarcity—as was the case with food—of medicines. Yet, in not few cases, many of those who believed in the "herbularyos" did get cured of whatever their actual ailments were. And a number of well-known folk medicines and practices are worth citing: boiled bark of "darita," a Tagalog name for a certain kind of tree, results in a very bitter liquid concoction, and drinking it as herbularyos prescribed helped many to recover from malaria. Daily cleansing of skin wounds and ulcers with a guava decoction produced out of boiling fresh guava leaves in fresh water proved effective in hastening healing. Then for dysentery and kidney trouble, daily drinking of a liquid concoction produced out of boiled leaves of "sambong" (a kind of herbaceous tree), was also a quack prescription that seemed effective.

And what is more, even "tawas"—a sort of diagnosis done not scientifically but by way of just some incantations followed by immersion of paper in a bowl of plain water—actually enabled the sick who got subjected to it to recover.

This is an episode told by an eye-witness. When a typhoid victim had already remained in bed for more than a week without showing any sign of recovering, his family decided to call for a "tawas"-conducting "herbularyo." As the quack doctor sat by the sick man's bedside, he requested that the family give him a bowl of plain water and three pieces of paper—of the kind used for hand-rolling cigarettes. After putting down the bowl of water on a chair, he uttered what sounded a prayer, and then immersed the papers, one after the other, in the bowl of water, taking time to first examine each paper before lifting it from the bowl. When he came to the third paper, on it, while in the bowl of water, appeared clearly—in an outline form curiously somewhat like that of photographed figures in a film's negative—the images of three diminutive children seated together underneath the bed of a man lying on it. Those in the family could only sigh out murmurings of wonder as they saw the unmistakable images on the paper, while the "herbularyo" said that certain spirits called "nono" in Tagalog were playing with the sick man.

Without prescribing any kind of medicine, the "herbularyo" just advised that, as remedy, the family "must make an offering to the spirits by way of placing a plate of food and a lighted candle on the floor, near the bed of the sick man and let both stay there overnight." To the family's great elation, the sick man did recuperate not long after this was done.

Whatever it was that actually restored the man's normal health, his family could only think of two things: 1) Their faith and the man's own might have helped; and 2) The man's natural body defenses might have somehow vanquished what infected him.

Another Eye-Witnessed Wartime Happening of Strange Nature

A young girl was with her family in a barrio, reorganizing their lives during the early part of Subic's occupation by the Japanese. The girl and her family were on a temporary stay in Subic's barrio of Balaybay at the time. They had recently relocated to it from their home in town, where food was scarce because of the conquering Japanese forces. The family's other relatives preferred staying behind in town, though, along with other newly resettled evacuees from the mountains. Simultaneously with the problem of food supply at the time was the sudden onset as well of widespread sicknesses that started taking a great toll on the life of town folks. And what aggravated the situation was the sudden undersupply, too, of medicines—thanks also to control of their availability by hordes of Japanese conquerors!

Now, one afternoon when the girl was sitting along with her family in a yard where there was a rattan hammock and a couple of outdoor bamboo beds called "papag" in Tagalog, she just suddenly looked at a street nearby and pointed to somebody not actually there while blurting as if in great surprise, "Ay, ayan si Tiyong Felicito! Ay, ayan si Tiyong Felicito!" In English, this translates, "Oh, there is Uncle! Oh, there's Uncle!"

She was not asleep, dreaming, but fully awake, and neither was she with any illness likely to predispose her to deliriums. But under the circumstance, whatever caused it all (local superstition terms it "pangitain") remains mystifying to this day: the girl's uncle, her mother's lone, young brother, named Felicito, eleven kilometers away in had unexpectedly died at the very same instant that she was acting as if she was actually seeing him, coming into the yard from the street, thereby making her point to him and blurt out his name!

Actually, there was no wonder of any sort at all regarding the cause of the girl's young uncle's untimely demise under the time's problematic circumstances. But why and how she just became suddenly aware of the latter's (physical? or spiritual?) presence and appearance (inferably) visible only to herself and not to any other family member in a setting of two different locations eleven kilometers apart could only be concluded about thus: It could veritably be a typical case of "spiritual telepathy" transmitted via the girl's inexplicable or inherent but (perhaps) undeveloped (psychic?) ability.

The girl, in her adulthood, still remembers clearly all about the mystifying matter. She has a name familiar to many Subicquenians: she is called Sit—actually Teresita Del Monte, now residing as a naturalized senior citizen in California.

Family Home Relocations

Not long after recovery from sickness tenably restored some degree of normalcy in the lives of families resettled in Subic from their mountain evacuation, need for a more stable day-to-day living in terms of surer food supply at all times compelled many of them to temporarily relocate to other places. As motorized land transportation became to be all but totally nonexistent at the time, travel depended largely on horse-drawn rigs or carabao (water buffalo)-drawn carts; if unavailable, walking was a last recourse.

When a family of seven vacated their home in the Subic poblacion and established temporary residence in Pamatawan, a barrio between the town and Castillejos to the north, they enjoyed—for some three months—not only a steady supply of basic food stuffs but also the vantage chance of having a plentiful daily supply of fresh carabao milk sold by neighboring farmers. This made the family resell whatever extra milk supply they could buy, with an oldest, lone son delivering it to town, daily.

Contained in common whisky-size bottles, up to six bottles could be sold every day. The most regular buyer was the 10-sibling Juico family of Wawandue. A member of it was to later become Olongapo City mayor, Amelia J. Gordon, the mother of the current Philippine Senator Richard J. Gordon.

Rosary Recitation Helps Dispel a Night's Eerie Sight

It was one of those nocturnal makeshift arrangements whereby a whole family—as sort of an exigency—had to sleep all together in their house's living room. The household head's periodical travel to other places for wartime food procurement necessitated that his family temporarily fend for themselves. They comprised five children left under the care of their mother with the companionship of her younger sister—in her early twenties. It was about midnight when, while sleeping together on a big mat laid on the floor with the children, the younger of the two adult siblings was suddenly awakened by the sound of a rocking chair, which she noticed to be moving to-and-fro, as silhouetted against the house's front shell window panes, whose semi-transparency let outside night light filter into the darkness of the living room. The chair's continuous movement simply was quite a goose flesh-causing sight indeed—what with no one seated on it! And there was no other plausible cause—like wind or earthquake—to which the vacant chair's rocking in the stillness of the night could reasonably be ascribed!

In a trembling, nervous voice, "Ate, Ate, it seems we are being visited by Tiya Elena!" the younger sibling could only exclaim, while she shook her elder's shoulder, waking her up. She was actually referring to an aunt who died at war's outbreak.

"Let's say the Rosary!" the children's awakened mother could only suggest. Neither held a Rosary, but they just started reciting the prayer they were wont to say on occasion.

Then, being curious about their prayer recitations amidst the silence of the night, the youngest of the children, about four years old, just called out "Mamang, Mamang!"—meaning "Mother, Mother!"—so that she created the impression that she was either awake or acting on impulse. And as she called, the chair's rocking stopped and—of all the unimaginable—concomitantly with her enunciation of "Mother, Mother!" It was then that the two siblings discovered that the child was sort of toying with the chair with her foot: she had made the chair rock simply by pushing up and down with her foot its semi-horizontal, arced, floor-touching support. With no heart to chide the child, the siblings could only give out uncontrollable laughs to themselves. Afterward they resumed their sleep for the rest of the night, leaving the thought that their Rosary recitation was what engendered their relief from fright.

Military Control of Community Life

For the control of town living, conquering Japanese soldiers immediately established their headquarters at Subic Bay's Olongapo Naval Arsenal. It had been abandoned as an aftermath of the USAFFE debacle at Bataan and Corregidor in 1942. A separate Japanese garrison, in addition to the one in the Olongapo arsenal, was also installed in Grande Island or Fort Wint. It aimed mainly to guard against sea-routed entry into or departure from Subic Bay by Japan's "enemies"—or "mis-elements" such as guerrillas, who were to later constitute a strongly unified underground resistance. They became referred to by their own nemeses, the Japanese themselves, as the Ganaps.

In Subic proper was put up a third garrison, reportedly manned by soldiers comprising both Japanese native citizens and Korean draftees. It was schematically maintained with utmost regimental strictness, for its locale was seen as being geographically favorable to hard-to-control anti-Japanese underground resistance. It was established not long after most of the Subic evacuees who hid in the mountains had already settled back home—but only heightened over time the underground resistance movement in the town.

For roughly three years, fear engendered by daily checkpoint operations, around-the-clock visibility of command post movements, and just-across-the-street proximity of soldiers' general-purpose barracks and the interrogation-incarceration complex combined to subjugate a whole community. In the Subic poblacion were commandeered two adjacent, private buildings—one with two floor levels used as main headquarters and the other with just a ground floor used as an interrogation-incarceration center. Dr. Virgilio Afable, who became, after the war, director of the Olongapo General Hospital and congressman for Zambales, owned the first building. (Its site eventually metamorphosed into what is now the Herman Guerrero residential-business compound) But the second building remained under its original ownership: the Gaudencia-Santiago family. It was later leased to business operators.

Checkpoint as Chief Means of Town Control

In a portion of the curve of the street between and near the Afable and the Santiago buildings was installed a checkpoint where a sentry was posted daily. The curve, which leads to all directions in town, tended not only to slow down all kinds of travel except walking, but it also served as a common converging point among travelers coming from or going into any direction reachable only by passage through the poblacion, which is traversed by only a singular thoroughfare with crisscrossing arterial streets.

By military mandate, all people passing by had to bow before any uniformed soldier manning the checkpoint as the very personification of a ruling Japanese authority. This applied to people alone or in groups, young (except babies) or old, on a bicycle or an animal-drawn rig or any other vehicle, for physical show of obeisance. Anyone who disobeyed was immediately addressed and hand-summoned by the sentry with shouts of "Kura Kura!"—the equivalent of "Come here! Come here!" in English. Disobedience was punished with outright, on-the-spot punishment: a slap on the face or the nape, kick on any part of the body, beating with the butt of a gun, or immediate arrest, depending on the circumstance.

If one's manner of bowing was improper, the person was forced to repeat the act without any punishment—but in a way acceptable to the sentry. "When once I was carrying on my head a 'bakol' (big basket without handles) full of vegetables for sale in the market, the sentry did not like my bowing with the load on my head," relates Josefa (Ipay) Flores Odias of Ilwas, now a retired teacher. "The sentry commanded that I first put down my basket before I make my bow to him. I was about 15 at the time."

Among males, an "open-waist" policy was imposed by having passers-by required to always have their shirts tucked in—as means of facilitating body inspection for hidden side arms. If aboard any means of transportation (vehicular travel became a rarity except among Japanese soldiers), passengers had to get down and bow before the sentry.

Methodical Projection of Ruling Forces' Constant Presence in Town

Whether or not it was by deliberate design, the Subic-garrisoned Japanese soldiers had their kitchen, dinning room, and bath drums put up in the Afable building in such a way that those cooking, eating, or taking a bath routinely projected that they were "all there always."

Their kitchen and dinning room were without walls on the side facing the town's main street, and this made passers-by always see activities going on inside. Their bath drums—with which they heated water almost up-to-the-rim to allow a bather to get fully immersed in—were always visible from the street as well. The water in each drum was unchanged between many bathers, as they used it one after the other.

For help, the soldiers relied on volunteer young boys for preparing and cleaning their kitchen, washing utensils and plates. No pay was given to the boy helpers, but at the most they were allowed to take home with them all scraps of food the soldiers allowed as a sort of remuneration. This arrangement smacked of oppressive treatment, but its no-choice aspect had somehow made it possible for up to five poor families to get saved from the debilitating perils of under-nourishment and hunger.

Japanese Incarceration-Torture Building

When Ganaps' pro-Japanese spying started ushering in arrests of persons suspected as guerrillas—particularly after people somehow got used to a semblance of a resettled yet insecure community living, the Santiago building came in quite handy. Its cement-floored room fronted the town's main street and faced on the right side a shore. (It is now the place where the new Subic Public Market stands.) It used to be a promenading area for fishermen and seaside residents. This was where arrestees were interrogated and incarcerated. There, many suspected and arrested guerrillas underwent untold hours of torture and agony while being investigated and being forced to reveal their peers' identities. The room's low windows did little to prevent passers-by from seeing or hearing how those investigated were subjected to shriek-producing torture—like prisoners' being whipped, hanged by their feet, or having fingernails, pulled out, to mention the most common. Contemporary eye-and-ear-witness accounts of goings-on in the room whenever guerrilla suspects got confined in it invariably reported that most of those investigated just found themselves instinctively crying out in agonizing, hellish, unbearable pain. Even the Japanese sentry posted nearby did not discourage curious passers by from watching the torture proceedings in the room. This was an indirect means of discouraging anti-Japanese underground resistance among town folks.

As it was, most of those investigated were actually guerrillas—and their arrest arose only because of Quisling Filipinos' traitorous finger-pointing. But the sadder scenario is that most of those who did get identified as such were executed.

Indirect Intimidation by Deliberate Shooting in Public

Obviously, to make people more fearful, one Japanese soldier sporadically made rounds of the town with his rifle to shoot down the first dog he met anywhere. With the soldier's bulky build and sharp-looking, slit eyes, extra frightening features, just the sight of him publicly aiming at wherever his canine target (he always seemed unmindful of potential harm to bystanders) proved scary to many! He notoriously became known by the name, Zuzuki, with his sadistic public shooting down of dogs wherever his whim took him to. He instilled a sense of morbid uneasiness in neighborhoods. To people he had learned to like, however, he managed to make himself amiably conversational in broken Tagalog or English.

His dog-shooting pastime had one benefit. If a killed dog happened to be healthy or meaty, he would just order bystanders to bring the dog to the town's Japanese headquarters—for subsequent butchering and a gourmet's table preparations; if otherwise, the dead animal was just left to whomever would want it—also for similar purpose.

INCEPTION OF CIVILIAN (PUPPET) GOVERNMENT

The Kalibapi Slogan as Lure for People's Shift of Allegiance

To convince the general public that civilian authority was what actually governing in the national, provincial, and municipal levels, a ruling structure was set up in 1943 whereby Filipinos directly served as officials and rank-and-file. But ultimate authority over the conduct of official business and every related activity in all echelons and branches of the government rested in the Japanese military. This lent an aura of collaboration per se on the part of all Filipinos under the government's employ. But there was no better option, and a contrary choice was simply to court self-martyrdom, imperilment of the lives of the people themselves, or national perdition.

Pragmatic compromise thus became the safest guiding rule under the circumstance. And where collaboration was subtly restricted to non-sacrifice of other people's welfare and interests while rendered service positively contributed to preservation of unperturbed community living without severance of ties with a growing underground resistance, the result simply proved immeasurably worthy. In other words, it simply was the exact opposite of the Ganaps' brand of collaboration, for theirs inevitably resulted in unnecessary loss of lives while their counterpart's role resulted in life preservation.

Thus, although many Subiquenians rendered public service under the aegis of a government set up by ruling Japanese soldiers, their brand of collaboration was by and large actually geared not to pursuing the latter's ends but bracing for General Douglas MacArthur's "I shall return" promise. An actual instance, not long after government civil service was restored nationwide with the Japanese in control, Subic's Elementary School principal, whose name was Mr. Mariano Echuverri, had asked five Grade V boys to sing a guerrilla-themed song in a program attended by parents. The song included the phrase, "Sa bundok, sa gubat, kami ay walang gulat!" or, in English, "In mountains, in forests, we are without fright!" Actually, the song was about how guerrillas were conducting themselves relative to secret instructive messages coming from General MacArthur—the mere mention of whose name simply remained central to a whole nation's unstinted and sustained link with a considered motherland.

When this particular episode in wartime Subic took place, the Japanese-conceived ploy for solidifying Filipino collaboration via the slogan "Kalayaang Independente ng Bagong Pilipinas" (under the acronym KALIBAPI), which means in English, "Independent Freedom for a New Philippines," was already in full swing. It aimed to inculcate—but actually only to no avail—into Filipino minds what Japan was actually after in their reign over the Philippines. In public meetings, this was expounded on with the participation of no less than General Artemio Ricarte himself, General Emilio Aguinaldo's similarly high-profile contemporary who never pledged allegiance to the U.S., unlike Aguinaldo himself at the end, when the U.S. took over Spain's rule over the Philippines in 1898. General Ricarte was flown all the way from Japan just to grace with his presence public meetings intended to trumpet out and promote the supposed attributes of "Kalibapi" in the manner of comparable political slogans, such as President Franklin D. Roosevelt's "New Deal," President Lyndon B. Johnson's "Great Society," President John F. Kennedy's "New Frontier," and President Ferdinand Marcos's "New Society."

And by a somewhat concrete gesture of showing that they were truly well meaning, Japanese soldiers themselves demonstrated real-life examples of paying respect to what in essence "Kalibapi" was to them. Martin Uson of Barrio Balaybay who once worked in a sawmill in the Japanese-controlled Subic Bay Naval Arsenal cutting lumber for construction of wooden-hulled ships relates: "We as lumber cutters routinely went to work with our IDs emblazoning the word KALIBAPI, and Japanese soldiers we met on the way always bowed to us once they see it worn on our chests. Our pay was half a ganta of rice a week plus some wartime-printed money, but it was in reality empty of intrinsic worth at the time—like their bowing to us!" He is now a resident of California.

On the economic side, agriculture or food production was particularly focused on, especially in central Luzon where the so-called rice granary of the Philippines thrived—the province of Nueva Ecija and its adjoining lowland plains. It was also emphasized as part of curriculum revisions in public secondary schools where agriculture or farming was a major subject or area of specialization.

Kalibapi's Concomintant Objectives

Aside from directing decisions on the national economy, the "Kalibapi"-fronted civil government, then headed nationally by Dr. Jose Laurel as president, also controlled all levels of public education. The Japanese authorities' purpose was to turn out future citizens engrained with statutorily required obedience to the Japanese government. In the elementary schools, Japanese teachers themselves handled classes for learning the fundamentals of Japanese reading, writing, and arithmetic. To facilitate pupils' learning counting numbers in Japanese, an exercise was held daily, and each movement was counted using the numbers, "itsi, ni, san, si, go," or "one, two, three, four, five," etc. The learning of the Japanese national anthem was a requirement in all elementary schools. If memory is correct, it begins with the words "Miyoto o kai…rak kit ti…" To casually establish rapport with young children, Japanese soldiers held bayonet duel drills where two children were clothed with body and face protective gear and allowed to practice hitting each other with the end of a long round-ended pole that was used as a simulated gun with fixed bayonet. Two soldiers stood and moved, demonstrating steps to follow, complete with the cry of, "Attack," "Atot-tot!" every time a thrust of the pole was made forward into the body of either of the supposed antagonists. The drills were held right within the compound of the Japanese headquarters' housed in the Afable building.

Price of Collaboration

While the great majority of those employed under the Kalibapi-dedicated government civil service never really developed any spirit of allegiance with the Japanese, a few chose to be the opposite. And those who did were simply identified with and categorized as Ganaps, with their pro-Japanese leanings being voluntary and undoubted. But some of them over-collaborated so that they became the most worrisome bane to members of the strongly anti-Japanese underground resistance, the guerrillas. Thus, under the circumstance, the Ganaps, be they officially Kalibapi-employed or just plain civilians but identified as actually pro-Japanese spies, became the targets of liquidation by guerrillas.

This was an actual, typical case. When incumbent Police Chief Fajardo died sometime in 1942 of sickness while in a mountain evacuation, his place was taken over—when the Japanese installed the Kalibapi municipal government in Subic on about the year after—by Ganap 2. To him and some designated wartime PC (Philippine Constabulary) forces was entrusted, by ruling Japanese authorities, the responsibility of directly maintaining peace and order in the Subic municipality. This was when the Subic underground resistance was growing.

But Ganap 2 happened to be a stickler for loyalty more to his Japanese masters than to his fellow Filipinos, in general, and co-Subiquenians, in particular. On a number of occasions when arrested guerrilla suspects were brought to him for routine interrogation, he hardly showed compunction in exacting confessions from them via physical torture he himself meted out to them. "He was the most brazenly pro-Japanese of all the Ganaps in Subic," relates Augusto De La Paz, once a guerrilla himself, who later became Subic's vice-mayor, now a naturalized U.S. senior citizen living in Hayward, California. "His actions showed he was a great danger to the lives of many guerrillas, so he was liquidated by a designated underground resistance triggerman from the Manila Hunters, and I just left the scene when he fell," De La Paz elaborated.

Actually, Ganap 2 was shot during a public dance held evening of June 8, 1943, at the Saint James Hall, which was to later get transformed into Subic's first high school run by private citizens in partnership with the Subic Catholic Church. In the incident, during which air-kerosene lamps were the vogue for a lightening system (in the lack of electricity), a bullet obviously ricocheted from the hall's concrete floor and hit Patricia Salang on her leg. She was one of many guests present in the occasion, and in later years she became principal of the Subic Elementary School. Two other Subiquenians wounded by stray bullets in the incident were Severino Salang of Calapandayan and and Ofelia Labrador of Ilwas. An eye-witness who well remembers the unforgettable wartime public assassination of a high local official was Maxima D. Tala of Wawandue, who was to later become a retiree of the Subic municipal government. "I saw the incident, too," narrates Josephina Bernal, now of Hayward, California, "and I was a teenager watching from the outside."

Another pro-Japanese spy who was liquidated by order of the Subic guerrilla command was Ganap 3. Popularly known as "Gulong-gulong," he was shot on the head about noon of a Sunday, right in Subic's former public market, which then was located at where the new Subic Municipal Hall now stands. Japanese soldiers and the Kempetai later arrived at the scene of the killing, which took place amid people doing their usual buy-and-sell business chores at the time, but their investigation was fruitless. Like Ganap 2's killing, it remained one of a much-talked-about Subic guerrilla exploit even after the war.

Aborted Third Liquidation Plan

A plan to liquidate another "dangerous" man next to Gulong-gulong was discussed in a decision-making meeting of the Subic guerrilla command when, by intercession of one of its field men employed in a school under the Subic Kalibapi-run municipal government, plan deferment "for further observation" was made a temporary option. The interceding guerrilla's wife was a cousin of the intended third liquidation target's wife, and the latter's being yet without a house of their own circumstantially found themselves accommodated in a space with their children in the house of the guerrilla's family.

Actually, the Subic guerrillas' intended third liquidation target was an in-law of the already liquidated Subic police chief. It was thought by them that with the police chief's liquidation, his in-law no longer had a strong temptation for sharing information detrimental to guerrillas. His disappearance from a position of power thus somehow fortuitously saved the neck of his relative from a taste of his own fate that they had contemplated but only later chose to forego. The liquidated police chief was then considered to be the greatest menace to the Subic guerrillas.

Male "Zonification" as Means of Curbing Guerrilla Activity

In their attempt to stop Subic's growing underground resistance, which started to build up strength shortly after May 1942, the Kempetai instituted a tactically dreaded scheme to better control civilian life. The Kalibapi-installed municipal government referred to it as "male zoning" ("sona" in

Tagalog). Aimed to inhibit and discourage males of battle age from consorting or joining with guerrillas, it consisted in the demarcation of Subic's barrios into zones with the objective of determining the number, identities, and personal circumstances of adult males in each zone. The zones were of such a size that keeping track of these males could be achieved with the highest possible degree of ease and reliability.

With the help of Ganaps—few dared to show their presence, the zones were subjected to procedural, sporadic visitations by Japanese soldiers to find out, within certain unannounced times, males staying at home or somewhere else. Those found not at home naturally became prone to suspicion—with certainty of their being automatically arrested once their whereabouts were determined. On the other hand, to whomever happened to be around on zoning time, the mere thought of their being arrested too—if circumstances caused them to be somewhere else, served as a deterrent to their joining with guerrillas.

Post-Zoning Incarceration of Rounded-Up Adult Males and Their Release

Sometime in 1944, six adult males in Balaybay, a barrio geographically sandwiched between the western metes of Subic and Castillejos, were arrested, their hands tied, and imprisoned in the Japanese garrison in Subic. Their arrest came about after they all happened to be not at home in the course of a "zoning" operation conducted by Japanese soldiers and a Kempetai. But interrogation failed to illicit the desired information from them. As was later credibly established, they all, as small farmers, were busy at the time they were "zoned," attending to their rice land preparation routines for the year's planting season, which often started in June. To the Japanese, any activity relating to agriculture was then vital, and this somehow helped make them decide on the "zoned" prisoners' immediate release.

Actually, though, they were supporters of guerrillas, who, at certain times, normally depended mostly on barrio farmers, as well as other folks known for a better status, for part of their food supply. For cigarettes, stores were the source of occasional handouts to guerrillas staying most of the time in hinterlands. Any information of this nature could be enough to result in the Kempetai's apprehension of anyone pointed to by Ganaps as guerrilla aid-givers, but it was clear under the circumstance that the released prisoners' arrest was attributable purely to their being not at home when "zoned."

Food Aid to "Zoned" Prisoners

Prior to the "zoned" prisoners' release, a Kalibapi government-appointed schoolteacher had learned that most of them were his relatives. In fact, one of them was his brother. Thus, despite only conjecturable repercussions and other related implications of the time's tensions, the teacher had exigently decided to send food (consisting of a basketful of boiled rice and "dining-ding" or vegetables cooked with salted fish and broiled fish in soupy mix) to them, with his 13-year-old son doing the errand.

After his son was allowed entry by a Japanese guard into the garrison's incarceration cell, practically all of the prisoners nearly came to tears as they saw him. He was known to most of them. Their arms were tied in front of them with ropes. As they ate the food he brought them with their untied hands, the teacher's brother could only mutter to his nephew, "The lunch they [the Japanese] gave to each of us consisted only of three spoonfuls of rice with two pieces of champoy!" (The word champoy refers to a kind of salted fruit.)

Related Facts on the "Zoned" Prisoners' Imprisonment Episode

In the months that followed, all the prisoners were to become active members of the underground resistance—and they had a particularly pressing causal reason. On January 17, 1945, guerrillas ambushed two truckloads of Japanese soldiers at a hilly, winding road (called Salungahin) mid-way between Subic and Castillejos. It resulted in the death of twenty-one soldiers and the wounding of eight others. After their commander learned from Ganaps that it was in the direction of Balaybay that the ambushers retreated to as remnant Japanese forces pursued them, the barrio was raided the next day by a replacement batch of soldiers. "A truck-mounted machine gun let loose a barrage of fire on the barrio, which they then burned down afterwards!" relates an eye-witness, Martin Uson, a Balaybay native now living in California.

A side fact to this actual wartime episode is that prior to the war, the teacher's brother, who was "zoned" with the Balaybay farmers and then released, had once operated a medium rice huller in Castillejos. He reported that the former mechanic, Ramon Magsaysay, who later became the highest and most famous guerrilla in Zambales and then president of the Philippines, was quite a neighborly guy who occasionally served as a consultant.

Kempetai's Cloak-and-Dagger Actions

And what is more—this time in the nature of a practically cloak-and-dagger scenario that ensued not long after the "zoned" farmers' release, a Kempetai, who had an alternate, began a routine of being always within the neighborhood of the residence of the teacher who sent his son to bring food to the "zoned" farmers while incarcerated in the Japanese garrison. It seemed the Kempetai was observing daily goings-on at the vicinity and right within the premises of the teacher's house. Under it actually then there truly was a hidden, underneath a pile of interspersing lumber, a guerrilla-issued rifle for the teacher's ready use as situations might warrant. To stave off what was seemingly an impending arrest and danger to his family, the teacher had perforce to relocate himself with his whole family to somewhere else at the first possible chance. It then had become established as a precedent that in almost every instance where a Kempetai maintained a daily presence in any neighborhood, what subsequently followed was arrest and immediate death to whoever was arrested thereat. And almost no Subiquenian guerrilla pointed out by the town's Ganaps escaped Kempetai attention and subsequent sure arrest.

The place to which the teacher relocated his family was some 100 kilometers away from Subic—in Wacon, Candelaria. Because of the time's rarity of long-distance transportation by land (trucks used charcoal and coconut shells to run steam-powered vehicles in Manila) he relied on an "outriggered parao" (schooner-type of sailboat) owned by Luis Quejado that sailed out of Subic Bay and cruised along the Zambales coast lining the eastern periphery of the China Sea, to almost the northern tip of the province.

But even if there already, far from a previously perturbing danger that dissipated in great relief found in the far, coastal isolation of a fishing barrio which other Subic families had also relocated to—the Favors, the Felicitases, the Daytos, and the Ocampos as the most familiar, he and his family, just as all the other barrio inhabitants, did not get spared of the burdens of sporadic, emergency evacuations. These occurred every time news got around that Japanese soldiers were on their way to the barrio for only one fearsome reason: a Japanese "zoning" raid and its uncertain aftermath.

Evacuations were always towards hinterland areas, at times across marshes and even in the middle of the night—all by foot with belongings carried on the head or the shoulders. These raids dislocated and intimidated families who were trying to undertake every means of self-protection. The Japanese became stricter in their control and treatment of civilians. Tensions then spawned by word-of-mouth-disseminated news on General Douglas MacArthur's having already returned and landed at Leyte in October 1944 along with his liberating U.S. forces accounted for the Japanese's sudden embarkation on a frenzied and seemingly vindictive fit of belligerence and hostility.

The Unique Scenario of a Fish That Was Caught by Its Tail

In Wacon at the time, "sapyaw," a kind of night semi-deep-sea fishing done by clan or volunteer hands with use of lead sinker-chained net and petromax light (out of kerosene-and-air-fed lamps), was the chief means of making a living. For the advantage of the system's generated illumination as spread out in the dark by its tandem of bright lamps, other fishermen operating individually by a common baited hook-and-line method were free to ply their skill at allowable vicinities. To everybody's great amazement one night, a patriarch of Subic's Felicitas family in evacuation in Wacon at the time luckily caught a fish almost the size of his own body—not by its mouth, however, but extraordinarily, by its tail! Proper technique, termed "pasotsot," required tiring the fish as it struggled in freeing itself and to help guard against this in favor of its lucky catcher, others using their own hook-and-line gear were discreet enough to pull out their own lines off the water for preventing multiple line entanglements, which could otherwise result in disappointments. When the fish finally lost its energy after less than half an hour or so, its overjoyed catcher easily managed to pull it out off the water with the aid of a wooden-handled iron hook—much to the congratulatory exclamations of "Ang suwerte ninyo!" or "You're very lucky!" as shouted almost in unison by other fishermen in their on out-rigged boats or "bancas." How the fish was caught by its (cartilaginous) tail, instead of its mouth, could only be remembered as simply one for Ripley's "Believe it or Not!"

Amnesty Offer for Surrendering Guerrillas

The inability of the Japanese military to totally put the Subic guerrillas under control made it decide on a grant of absolute amnesty to "all those who would voluntarily surrender and lay down their arms" as a gesture of allegiance to the Japanese government—via cooperation with the Kalibapi-installed municipal authority. This was communicated to the general public through posted written notices and barrio-to-barrio "bando"—or announcing services of a municipal town crier. In Subic at the time, the town crier was known as "Mang Simo."

The Japanese's amnesty offer was also offered through the services of Ganaps. Surrender was openly accepted starting in December 1942 in the campus of the Subic Elementary School. But only a handful of guerrillas did surrender, and the great majority of them did not but preferred to hold onto their arms, instead, until the U.S. liberation of Subic in January 1945.

Before the surrender event took place, a series of meetings were secretly held among guerrillas, determining in advance as to who would surrender and who would remain otherwise. From a tactical standpoint, the occasion was worthless to the Japanese but useful to the Subic guerrilla command. Those who surrendered remained loyal to the guerrilla cause, and it was only their love for their families that actually accounted for their voluntary surrender. For those who made a contrary decision, all what they simply needed to do was to care for all weapons issued to them and "carry on with the fight," in their own words.

Another advantageous result of the amnesty's consummation from the guerrillas' viewpoint was that all the Ganaps who openly took part in the surrender proceedings had self-disclosed their identities, as well as their being really rabidly pro-Japanese. This resultantly made for innovations in their underground activities, one being the induction of female guerrillas whose duty was mainly to spy on the movements of not only Japanese soldiers but also every known Ganap and in and out of town. Also, close female relatives of guerrilla officers were tasked to help cook food for men under their command. "I was in the company of Cody, the wife of Captain Jose dela Paz, Jr., and her mother-in-law," relates Naty Ramirez, who was to later become the wife of guerrilla Lt. Augusto dela Paz, "in cooking food for the Hunters guerrillas in the mountain while they were conducting drills among themselves."

ADAPTATIONS TO WARTIME'S RESTRAINTS ON COMMUNITY LIVING

Predominant Forms of Recreation

Boxing was at the time the primary sports spectacle community folks' leisure was used for. It was in two categories: professional boxing staged up to twice a year inside a ring, and casual boxing held sporadically in neighborhood yards.

The Subic Saint James Hall, which had an elevated stage about four feet high above its ground floor, was where professional bouts were always held. Participated in by competing pugilists from all over Zambales, it attracted a large crowd of enthusiasts composed mostly of men, both old and young.

Fighters' motivations stemmed mainly from quest for fame, not necessarily for cash prize. The money of the time was nothing more than worthless tokens without any governmental guarantee. It was largely for this reason that although cockfighting was the number-one, favorite kind of betting-spurred sport among Filipinos, it saw relegation to a level of importance of anything but total oblivion throughout the era.

The boxers who became particularly famous for their feat not as repeat winners but as artful, speedy or hard-hitting fighters were Kid Balete, Jack Hammer, Fighting Cruz, and Fighting Taran. Not long after Subic's liberation by U.S. forces in 1945, Kid Balete fell to Philippine Constabularies' bullets when he attempted to fight with them in his post-war outlaw life. On the other hand, Jack Hammer joined with the U.S. Navy, and chose to reside permanently in San Diego, California, with his family upon his retirement.

To some of the Japanese soldiers assigned in Subic at the time, boxing exerted a strong appeal. But most of the time they watched bouts staged not in a ring but those of casual nature held among voluntary adolescent and even adult protagonists. In fact, they themselves at times offered to wear gloves and take on willing opponents—but actually only for tryouts.

An actual instance of this once saw a robustly built Subiqeunian guy named Julian Lim pitting himself against a challenging Japanese soldier (in civilian clothes). As the latter started receiving hits but hardly landing any on his opponent, he tried to shift to jujitsu by acts of removing his gloves and taking hold of his opponent's arms and body. Using his head, Lim right there and then raised both of his arms and said to the Japanese, in a friendly manner with an apparently forced smile on his face: "I give up; really; you'd defeat me!"

Government-issued "Mickey Mouse" money was actually a "forced legal tender" at the time. It hardly inhibited gambling with its use for bets, though. And the time's most popular kind of gambling, Bingo, was more of a pastime than a means of raking up money, since the money was virtually useless anyway. Held almost every day in practically all of Subic's bigger neighborhoods where people had not much to do, it was engaged in mostly by the common people, men and women, old and young alike.

The era's other gambling-tinged forms of recreation and pastime indulged in by both adults and adolescents were mainly mahjong, pool (akin to a billiard game but with use of flat and round wooden pieces instead of ivory balls), and common card games like blackjack and lucky nine.

Family and Adult Entertainment

Circus, which was termed also "zarzuela," consisting mainly of miscellaneous acrobatics or trapeze skills without animal participation, was the time's most common kind of entertainment patronized and enjoyed by families. Performers came from Manila and its suburban areas. In some instances, magic was included along with musical-comedy numbers. Space used was interchangeably that of the Subic old public market and the warehouse-type building (was to be later owned by Subic's Ong family) at its northeastern vicinity, depending on contracted pre-arrangements.

On certain occasions, a number of the performers, like one called "Bibon" who exhibited extraordinary physical strength by bending iron bars none of his kind could duplicate, were actually guerrilla intelligence agents assigned to gather information intended for General MacArthur's headquarters in Australia. "Bibon" is actually a Tagalog term for a high-speed banca, and its use by Bibon, the wartime stage performer was thought to be an undercover name.

Aside from circus as an occasionally held event for family entertainment, dancing in a cabaret was also held on weekends—but only among men, however. And even Japanese soldiers as well as forces of the Kemptai themselves were enthusiastic patrons.

Small-Time Means of Earning a Living

Despite its worthlessness, earning Japanese occupation money was simply necessary for family sustenance. Making glasses—one kind of an economic good—out of ordinary bottles was one cheap way of making a living. This was done with use of a thick, circle-looped wire that was heated and then put around a bottle that was afterwards immediately immersed in water to remove the unneeded upper half portion. Subsequent smoothening of the resultant glass product with file or whetstone finally resulted in drinking glasses sold in the market for income.

As remedy for the prohibitive price of kerosene used for home lamps, coconut oil lamps—which allowed concomitant use of water on which oil floats (to permit utilization of even tall bottles with broad open ends)—became more preferred in most homes at the time. The lamp's working principle was no different from that of a kerosene lamp, except that the wick of the former with oil as fuel was made to work with the aid of a cork that made it possible for the wick to normally keep on burning with fuel level constantly seen. Making of coconut oil lamps as a handicraft was one lucrative means of making a living at the time.

In Subic Bay at the time, two kinds of seaweed particularly valued for their good food value abounded each year. Gatherers sold them for income, and in the market they were called "ar-ar-osip" and "bal-balulang."

In the town's rural areas also abounded every month of May until June a certain kind of beetle called "abal-abal" or "abaw." Gatherers cooked beetles caught in baskets in quantity with improvised pepper-based attractants, and—as the product proved to really taste good to most people, they enjoyed some income from catching and selling the insect. Other small-time means of making a living engaged in by people at the time included "lambanog"—making or production of whisky from distilled "sasa" or nipa wine, hand-weaving of "pinokpok" or cloth out of abaca or maguey fibers, and making of sugar-coconut-based tuber and corn cakes.

The worthlessness of the era's Japanese-circulated money really did not deter people from embarking on any feasible business, and any kind of it somehow helped a lot in overcoming their war-shaped fate of economic hardships. Going on with life by all means simply necessitated the exchange of goods among them, and the use of even a worthless money as a medium for it was really an inevitable, no-other-choice option under the circumstances. As a result, inflation weirdly escalated to a point where money paid for what was bought with it had to be handed out in a bulky bunch for any commodity sold in exchange.

BIRTH AND OPERATIONS OF THE SUBIC UNDERGROUND RESISTANCE

Purpose and Related Activities

The Japanese's sordid treatment of USAFFE POWs, actual accounts of which preceded their arrival at Subic, was what seeded the town's underground resistance. In turn, the ingratiation of Ganaps with conquering

Japanese soldiers enabled the latter to learn of Subic's budding guerrilla force, and to control it was what triggered, partly or wholly, their establishment of their two-building garrison with an adjunct sentry shed in the town.

Different resistance groups initially came into existence in Subic, but later got unified under a shared common purpose: upkeep of fighting until the return of General Douglas MacArthur, whose secret radiograms sent to trusted guerrilla officers kept the spirit of resistance strongly alive all through the three-year Japanese rule of the town. Sabotage, intelligence gathering, aid in the escape of USAFFE and guerrilla prisoners, ambuscades, liquidation of dangerous pro-Japanese spies, and participation in battles pursued by U.S. liberating forces against retreating Japanese soldiers were what the Subic guerrillas mainly carried on from 1942 through 1945.

Beginnings

An American was actually the one who initiated underground resistance in Subic against its Japanese conquerors. In the middle of one night at Subic's outskirts, a U.S. Marine officer named Howard Moore, who escaped from captivity and surrender by the USAFFE at Bataan on April 9, 1942, happened to get in touch with Subicquenian Francisco Mendigorin. That meeting led them to Subic's hinterland barrio Nibangon, where, through Francisco Molina, they proceeded to see Numeriano Flores, a past Subic mayor, Eduardo Lesaca, a pre-war school teacher, Cecilio Esteban, incumbent Subic mayor, and Luis Afable, a businessman.

The group agreed to organize a guerrilla force for Subic. As their jurisdictional area of command, all Subic's southern barrios—Calapandayan, Calapacuan, Matain, Hulong Matain, and Naugsol, were assigned to Flores; all northern barrios—Baraca or the poblacion, Wawandue, Asinan, Mangan-Vaca, Aningway, and Pamatawan, to Lesaca. Flores and Lesaca later assumed the rank of captain under the Subic guerrilla command started by U.S. Marine Lt. Moore.

First Subic Guerrilla Casualty

Ganaps' finger pointing was the greatest single problem to the Subic guerrilla force right at the beginning. It resulted in almost every apprehension of, and 90 percent death to, whatever guerrilla fell victim to their traitorous quest for power. In Subic, the first guerrilla fatality caused by the exploits of the unpatriotic Ganaps was Lt. Moore himself. He was suddenly captured and executed outright by the Kempetai sometime in early 1943. The fact that Subic's underground resistance was yet in its formative stage with much to be learned, especially with respect to countering Ganaps' menace accounted greatly for Lt. Moore's short-lived fight against a widely hated enemy.

Although his death was a great loss to the Subic guerrilla command, from it was nevertheless wisely derived a valuable lesson: The guerrillas realized the urgent need for neutralizing Ganaps' danger, and it was to be done in such a way as would preclude Japanese retaliation without loss of civilian lives. Killing of Japanese would be avoided according as situations warranted but not killing of Ganaps, who, after all, were popularly known as traitorous. To forestall guerrilla growth, "Ten civilian deaths by decapitation for every one Japanese death perpetrated by guerrillas" was what the Kempetai then had fashioned as a Sword-of-Damocles warning to the general public at the time.

Thus, assigning of spies and deep penetration agents out of carefully selected guerrillas including adult females started in the wake of Lt. Moore's death. It was a plan not 100% effective, but it was all that could be relied upon as an antidote for the danger posed by Ganaps to guerrillas themselves. With time it developed as a consensus that when two Subic Ganaps got liquidated earlier then, there were those of their kind that somehow relaxed on their finger-pointing activities as fifth columnists or Filipino Quislings.

Other Americans in the Subic Underground Resistance Movement

Another American who initiated and led the organization of covert resistance against the Japanese not only in Subic but also all over Central Luzon was Lt. Col. Claude Thorpe, a USAFFE officer who excluded himself from the USAFFE surrender in Bataan on April 9, 1942. He gathered USAFFE stragglers like himself and with them established their general headquarters at Mount Pinatubo on the mountainous Pampanga-Zambales border. Despite his capture and eventual execution by the Kempetai in late 1942, still another American, known as Capt. Ralph McGuire, put up a separate guerrilla command in Western Luzon, a geographical part of which constitutes the whole Zambales province itself. But sudden misfortune wrought by the Kempetai y led to Capt. Mcguire's capture and subsequent execution, too. Thereafter, from the deaths of illustrious American guerilla leaders emerged other comrades-in-arms for a take-over, and one who opted to establish his own separate command was Capt. John Boone.

Emergence of Hunters ROTC Guerrillas

In March 1943, two representatives of the Manila-based Hunters ROTC Guerrilla Command arrived at Matain, a coastal barrio of Subic some four miles from Olongapo, in the company of Benito Novales, a native Subciquenian. Both looking able-bodied with a he-man physique, they were Captains Leonardo Aquino and Amado Santos, and their mission was to procure arms and ammunition, and organize a G-2 or intelligence unit in Subic, by authorization of Col. Eleuterio "Terry" Magtanggol, overall commandant of the Manila-headquartered Hunters ROTC Guerrillas, who in later years became defense secretary under President Ramon Magsaysay. The two Hunters' visit was to later prove dramatically fruitful.

At the time, Eduardo Lesaca had to relocate—to avoid capture by the Kempetai—to Manila with his family; he turned over his command to Jose dela Paz, Jr., more popularly called "Peping." As one appointed—by Aquino—Chief G-2 for Zambales, dela Paz, who then adopted the alias "Joseph Paterno," concomitantly emerged Subic Sector Commander of the Hunters ROTC guerrillas. In late April 1943, he had his guerrilla outfit absorb all other guerrillas actively affiliated with the Mcguirre Western Luzon Guerrilla Command, which included Aetas. Also inducted as Hunters' affiliates were Captains Numeriano Flores and Eduardo Lesaca, as well as one Lt. Enrique Vindua. They all were to later prove quite instrumental in controlling robberies, banditry, and cattle-rustling in Subic.

The Hunters' Initial Underground Daredevil Action

Sometime in May 1943, a group of Hunters boarded a small oar-power banca and secretly rowed out of Subic Bay for Mariveles, Bataan. Their mission: to barter rice for whatever arms and ammunition they could avail themselves of from the forces of a fellow guerrilla named Captain Briones. They accomplished this amid great risk of being caught by the Japanese, who had garrisons in Morong, Bagac, Saysayin, three coastal barrios of Bataan, and in Fort Wint itself at the mouth of Subic Bay. They had brought back with them a few rifles and automatic arms.

They made a second trip to Mariveles after securing a few more sacks of rice from guerrilla supporter Don Fausto Nepomuceno. They had obtained additional arms and ammunition—but at a great extra cost: While traveling on foot in the hills of Mariveles, four of them were spotted and killed by Japanese patrols. They were Lt. Maximo Lacambra and Privates Gregorio Atienza, Eduardo Mirasol, and Santos Timaan.

Silver Lining Behind a Cloud of Comrades' Death

The four Hunters' tragic death was deeply mourned by their comrades-in-arms, but sorrow behind it got somehow soothed, if not compensated for, by a certain piece of news gladdening to everyone: In July 1943, Aquino, who left Subic a captain, was sent back to Subic with the rank of major by Col. Magtanggol, and he had brought with himself things not ordinarily seen in Zambales or anywhere else: magazines from Australia, carbines and ammunition, and other stuffs showing proofs of contact with the outside world. Jubilance was everywhere and the underground resistance members felt simply more solidly unified than ever.

Organization of Hunters Unit Outside Subic

By order of Colonel Terry Magtanggol of the Manila General Headquarters of the Hunters Guerrillas, a separate Hunters unit was organized in Maloma, Botolan. The unit's chief organizer was Manuel Barretto, who became in later years Zambales governor. To gauge overall reliability of the Maloma Hunters guerrilla force he formed, Major Leonardo Aquino and Captain Amado Santos, relying on and with an entourage of Subic Hunters officers comprising Lt. Leopoldo Afable (who was interim mayor of Subic at the time), Lt. Luis Afable, Lt. Marvin Buendia, Lt. Benito Novales, and Capt. and Chief G-2 Jose dela Paz, went to Maloma for evaluative inspection. Their findings: Barretto did well in having forged a solid underground resistance force out of able-bodied men willing to fight at all cost.

Training in Manila Secret School of Hunters

On their way back to Manila, Major Aquino and Capt. Santos had twelve Subic Hunters leave Subic and go with them. Headed by dela Paz, who earlier had shipped out to the Manila-based Hunters GHQ sixty rifles, twelve pistols, and one Tommy gun using the truck of Luis Afable who "knew all requisites of the whole operation," the other eleven Hunters were to undergo specialized training in sabotage work, demolition, and special attack tactics. The result of their training was to eventually get tested first on what became a deathless raid not against Japanese soldiers but fellow Filipinos under Japanese employ.

Hunters' Raid on Subic Police and Philippine Constabulary Forces

On the night of January 4, 1944, the twelve Subiquenian guerrillas who underwent training at the Manila Hunters School formed the main attack team that raided and disarmed all of the police and Philippine Constabulary forces while quartered at their barracks near the old Subic Municipal Building. The raid was led by Maj. Aquino and Capt. Dela Paz, and—as planned—did not result in any death among those raided nor among the raiders themselves. All the policemen and the constabulary soldiers were taken prisoners, and the chase put into action by Japanese soldiers who arrived at the scene later was fruitless. Thereafter, Aquino went home to Manila and left the Hunters in Zambales under the command of Barretto in Botolan and dela Paz in Subic.

Then on a night in late January 1944, an American, Master Sgt. Clinton B. Wolf, arrived at the hideout of dela Paz. He had crossed over the Zambales mountain ranges from Bataan, after being separated from Capt. Daniel Boone during a raid by the Japanese in their camp. On his declared intention to serve with the Hunters, he was inducted into it with the rank of captain. Also designated general adviser and operations coordinator, Capt. Wolf served with the Subic Hunters until the liberation of Zambales by American GIs in January 29, 1945. In this capacity he maintained his command in divergent hideouts in the Subic's hinterlands, one of which was called Nalinang. "There, food was delivered to him by his Filipina wife named Gracing, and his group was periodically visited by guerrilla Lt. Augusto dela Paz on horseback," narrates Naty Ramirez dela Paz.

Hunters' Chance Confrontation with Philippine Constabulary Forces

Control of cattle rustling also occupied the Subic Hunters' attention at the time. When on one occasion some Hunters were on their way to apprehend bandits responsible for carabao rustling in a hinterland grazing area, they were intercepted by a group of constabulary men at the Pamatawan foothills. At the time, the biggest owner of a carabao herd, known to number up to about eighty heads that grazed daily within the flat fields of Pamatawan, was the Hilario family of San Roque, Castillejos. Bringing the herd back to their corral in Castillejos from Pamatawan usually created such a thick traffic of the slow-footed animals that dust filled up the air as they trudged heavily through the unpaved portions of the road from Pamatawan to Castillejos. Only one to two men usually pastured the animals every day at the vicinities of Pamatawan, so that stealing a head or two of them even on daytime tended to be not hard to do. After the family head, Inocencio Hilario, had divided his animal stock among his five children, pasturing the animals in large groups gave way to tending separate groups of just more than ten heads per group, making pasturing easier. But this did not deter occasional stealing of the animals by bandits.

And there had been instances where even Japanese soldiers had taken by force carabao heads owned by farmers. An eye-witness account of this was narrated by Cecilio P. Hilario, Jr., a retired USN sailor from Castillejos but now residing in Vallejo, California, thus: "My father was once hit on the head by a Japanese soldier when he refused to give away the carabao being forcibly taken from him! I was still then a young boy helping pasture our carabaos at the time."

That Pamatawan happened to have extensive grazing lands simply had made itself a favorite site for carrying out wartime animal thievery. Thus, as the intercepting all-Filipino constables and the Hunters faced one another at Pamatawan, a quick maneuver by Hunters Benito Novales, Victor Lacambra, and Zoilo Canlas got the constables surrounded by other Hunters ready to shoot nearby. This forced the constables to lay down their arms at the Hunters' demand. But as both opposing forces were about to leave, shouts made by some of the constables were heard by a group of Japanese soldiers, forcing the Hunters and their prisoners to retreat into the depths of the mountains in the direction of Balaybay.

Inception of Hunters' Intelligence Reports to Australia

On early September 1944, a certain Sgt. Cawagdan, a Filipino who was later learned to have set foot again in Philippine soil after a trip from Australia by a U.S. submarine that dropped him off at the coast of Tayabas, Quezon province, came to Matain looking for the head of the Subic underground resistance. Escorted by Capt. Sia, he was first received by Hunters Benito Novales and Jose de Perio. His immediate need was to see "Maj. Flash." Actually, he was referring to Col. Edward S. "Ding" Johnson, an Olongaponian founder and executive officer of the ZMD who suffered the sad fate of seeing his son and a brother included in the arrest of fifty-two guerrilla suspects who were tortured and then beheaded by the Kempetai in 1942 in Olongapo.

A day later, after Sgt. Cawagdan's meeting with Col. Johnson, a conference was held with dela Paz invited for multilateral planning of ways by which to relay intelligence reports to Australia. It happened that movements by aircraft in the San Marcelino airstrip and ships in and out of Subic Bay were worth focusing attention on for intelligence reporting, and Sgt. Cawagdan chose to establish his transmission point at Aglao, a hinterland area of San Marcelino, which is the third town from Subic, next to Castillejos.

His radio transmitting equipment was actually near the headquarters of another guerrilla group headed by Col. Merrill, an American USAFFE.

To a certain extent, even the mere thought that there now existed a visible means by which movements of the Japanese as a sworn enemy could be made known to higher authorities in Australia for proper decision-making purposes proved inspiring for the whole Subic underground resistance force. "The boys simply couldn't help relishing the thought that they form a very substantial part of the whole scenario of avenging their compatriots' sacrifice at Pearl Harbor, Bataan, and Corregidor," was a strongly unifying sentiment among the guerrillas themselves, their divergent units of commands notwithstanding.

Results of Intelligence Report to Australia

Sometime in 1944, a steady sailing of Japanese surface craft in small convoys along the Zambales coast facing the China Sea was seen by Luis Nepomuceno, a Hunters guerrilla assigned to observe any ship movements in Subic Bay. This was reported to Jose dela Paz, who in turn had it checked. After positive verification, it was relayed to Sgt. Cawagdan in Aglao. Two days later, U.S. planes bombed the convoy of ships sailing off the coast of Zambales. Japanese casualties included a heavy cruiser sunk, along with two big oil tankers and several transport ships.

Told that some survivors were sighted to be swimming towards a shore, dela Paz ordered Novales to lead a rescue team. A Briton and some Chinese were rescued. They were war prisoners, and all of them looked emaciated, with skeletal appearance. One simply couldn't help pitying the survivors for the sight they posed of themselves under the circumstance, as well as feeling angry at the hellish treatment their captors subjected them to. By their own words, they were meted out a punishment of slow death by torture and starvation. Their rescuers took them all to camp for whatever extent of nursing care the time's hardships could allow for their welfare. Due to the great suffering they experienced at the hands of their merciless captors, some of them manifestly went crazy. One even committed suicide in a fit of madness.

Cost of Raid on Convoy

Two U.S. planes were downed by anti-aircraft during the raid on the convoy of Japanese ships along the Zambales coast. One crashed and burned on a mountain, while the other fell into Subic Bay. A pilot was seen emerging from the fallen plane, but he happened to be heading towards a shore of a sitio, which—known to be exclusively inhabited by hardcore pro-Japanese spies, was called "Little Tokyo"—a war-stigmatized lair of Sakdals/Ganaps.

Impetus in Hunters' Underground Derring-do Action

By mid-December 1944, the Subic guerrillas heightened their Japanese-eradication actions.

The frequency of U.S. airplane raids conducted in Luzon and Zambales made everyone feel that Gen. MacArthur's return right in Luzon was nearing, and this anticipation emboldened the Hunters to hanker for more fighting against the Japanese. But their undertaking of it was to end with disappointing results. After a covert reconnaissance visit at Grande Island led directly by dela Paz on December 11, 1944, a squad of School of Hunters-trained saboteurs was assembled two days thereafter, on December 13; their mission: to set fire to and destroy Fort Wint's oil-gasoline reservoir and its lighthouse.

Led by Victor Lacambra and Zoilo Canlas at midnight, the saboteurs, riding in a banca, were split into two groups. The first succeeded in burning the fuel depot and the second, the lighthouse. But they were unfortunately spotted in their acts by Japanese guards, whose barrage of gunfire forced them to save their own dear lives by swimming the whole breadth of Subic Bay's expanse covering the distance from the fort to Matain—about three miles or about five kilometers. Fortunately under the darkness of the night, they suffered no untoward incident whatsoever—until the next morning.

In the early hours of the morning of December 14, 1944, Japanese soldiers suddenly arrived at Matain and rounded up all its male inhabitants. Arrested outright on the spot, all of them were brought to and incarcerated in the Japanese garrison in Subic.

Benito Novales had learned in advance of the raiders' arrival, but the lack of appropriate telecommunication equipment and the impossibility of individualized person-to-person monitoring under the circumstance inhibited his giving of a warning on time. End result: Hunters Hilarion Enriquez, Antonio Morales, and Leopoldo Tamoria were executed—they sacrificed their lives for the destroyed fuel reservoir and lighthouse in Fort Wint. The rest of the prisoners were released, but thenceforth became tagged for tighter "zoning."

Tightened Japanese Soldiers' Hold on Maloma

The Japanese's learning of Hunters' operations in Maloma led them to also conduct a surprise raid on it on December 14, 1944. But they had in their company this time constabulary men. And their foremost quarry was Manuel Barretto, the Maloma Hunters' commanding officer. But the Japanese-Filipino-teamed raiders missed by about ten minutes seeing Barretto, who had earlier left coincidentally for Subic in the company of fellow Hunters Rosendo Soriano and Benito Novales. Either by sheer intuition (or what not?), Barretto simply sensed that he definitely was a most wanted man in Maloma. So, he just thought it wise to stay for some time in the company of his fellow guerrillas in Subic.

Japanese Miss Another Chance for Supposedly a High-Priced Capture

While in Subic, Barretto took time out to wait for some cooling off in the Japanese's ongoing manhunt for him. Then, in anticipation of an earlier pre-arranged rendezvous with a U.S. submarine off a mid-Zambales coast, he insisted that on his trip back home to Maloma dela Paz ought to go with him. The reason was obvious to all: the anticipated rendezvous could mean tidings exchange consequential in every respect to a commonly shared cause of ensuring defeat of the Japanese at the least sacrifice of resources—both human and materiel.

Both Barretto and dela Paz actually had barely left when all of sudden Japanese soldiers just arrived seemingly from nowhere for dela Paz's apprehension.

Consolidation of Guerrillas' Command by Capt. Ramon Magsaysay

"In a meeting held by various guerrilla groups, we had voted that our overall guerrilla commander in Zambales should be Ramon Magsaysay," was what August dela Paz, the guerrilla who became Subic vice-mayor but now is a naturalized U.S. citizen living in California, narrated of his having met with the man who became, first, defense secretary, then, Philippine president. Incidentally, the narrator is one of the three brothers of Capt. Jose "Peping" dela Paz

On January 4, 1945, some three weeks before American GIs liberated Subic from three multi-hardship-laden years of Japanese occupation, Capt. Magsaysay invited Capt. dela Paz, among other creditable underground resistance leaders, to a meeting. Its purpose: to consolidate Zambales's various guerrilla groups under a unified command known as the Luzon Guerrilla Forces. Sensing pursuit of love of country rather than personal glory as dela Paz's strongest motivation behind his guerrilla exploits, Capt. Magsaysay appointed him commanding officer of the Subic Guerrilla Sector, to operationally function under the Luzon Guerrilla Forces—the main, sizable underground entity enjoying Gen. MacArthur's full recognition, as were duly accredited others.

For the appointment, dela Paz and his second brother, Placido, who was more popularly known as "Ceding," nearly got captured—and even killed—by the Japanese! On their way to the meeting called for by Capt. Magsaysay, dela Paz and his brother were jointly riding a horse. They happened to be seen by Japanese soldiers aboard a truck, and so were pursued up to where the truck could travel the road safely. The place that confronted the pursuing Japanese happened to have a terrain too inaccessible to motorized travel, and this simply spelled out a safe getaway in the dela Paz brothers' favor.

Pre-U.S. Liberation Intensified Guerrilla Actions

Mid-January 1945 started seeing frenzied movements not only by Subic's guerrillas but also its civilian population. Reason: U.S. liberating forces' landing was about to take place in Zambales. As one in charge of intelligence reporting in Zambales, Calixto Relente did a creditable job dealing with the disposition of all known Japanese forces maneuvering in Zambales. Based on this, Magsaysay took immediate action to ensure that rolling stocks, communications facilities, and all other major aspects of the Japanese's warring capacity be sabotaged by every possible means. His order to this effect was relayed to the field with the message, "As per radiogram sent by Gen MacArthur!"

Pursuant to this order, two truckloads of Japanese soldiers were ambushed on January 16, 1945, in Subic's outskirts. Led jointly by Captains dela Paz, B. Ibanez, and Alfredo Codilla, with some ROTC men from the University of the

Philippines and some Negritos recruited by them forming the main fighting force, the guerrillas totally destroyed, by burning, one truck and killed six Japanese soldiers and their captain. The other truck was able to get away. This spurred a retaliatory raid by the enemy on Naugsol, one of Subic's hinterland barrios.

In the Naugsol raid, thirty guerrillas were captured. But this was not all. Reprisals by the Japanese began to take on such severe form that civilians were forced to relocate or once again seek refuge in the mountains.

Deadliest Ambush Against Traveling Japanese Soldiers

On January 17, 1945, after underground advice to civilians showed a willingness to evacuate again to the mountains or elsewhere, the Subic guerrillas launched a daytime ambush against some truckloads of Japanese soldiers on their way to the San Marcelino airstrip. The operation was executed in Salungahin, a mountainous area traversed by a winding, slow-grade road with some ravines between Subic and Castillejos—with San Marcelino being northwardly the next town to the latter. Under the ambushing guerrillas' really commanding, vantage position as made possible by their being in a higher elevation overlooking their target below, they had killed twenty-one enemy soldiers and seriously wounded eight others. Also, they had immobilized two trucks. Two guerrilla teams, each led by Capt. Lesaca and Capt. Dela Paz, accounted for the successful ambush—the deadliest ever in Subic—and without any casualty on the ambushers' side.

Retaliatory Steps Taken by Survivors of the Salungahin Ambuscade

On the day following the Salungahin ambuscade, Japanese soldiers fanned out to Subic's outskirts and indiscriminately fired machine guns towards practically all of the town's mountainsides. Their strafing operations, which lasted for hours, were so thorough that one guerrilla was fatally hit: Sgt. Juan Tiong, a brother of Benito Tiong, once a prosperous rice merchant owning a truck for his business.

A few days later, or on January 26, 1945, Japanese soldiers also conducted a surprise raid on the interior homestead areas of Manggahan (also called Mangan-Vaca), one of Subic's farming barrios Their raid bagged Capt. Lesaca and his brother Lt. Godofredo Lesaca. Once earlier, Ganap first finger-pointing nearly resulted in their joint arrest, too, but sheer luck had made them leave a few minutes before the supposed arresting Japanese soldiers arrived at the place pointed to by the Subiquenian Japanese spy, whom they well knew. This time, they were not lucky. They were both captured then taken to the Olongapo Naval Arsenal, where they were confined in the old, three-story, Spanish-vintage building which the Japanese used partly as prison. At the time, all the Japanese garrisoned in Subic town had already abandoned their posts and transferred to the Olongapo Naval Compound to join with their main forces there.

For the two captive guerrilla brothers from Subic, meanwhile, agents were sent to Olongapo to look into the possibility of rescuing them. But expectations of sure peril to all involved if any attempt was made at the time forestalled its materialization.

Day Two from Subic's Relief of the Yoke of Fear of Japanese's Rule

It was January 27, 1945, when Capt. Dela Paz received a memo from Capt. Magsaysay, advising about the need for immediate "pick-up of carbines, ammunition, hand grenades, and medicines dropped by American planes." With Col. Merrill's being at Aglao as a guerrilla lair nearest the pick-up point, the task was entrusted to him. Now, with additional materiel bolstering the Subic guerrilla command's ordinance, dela Paz was ordered to blow up the bridges at Matain and Maquinaya and place barriers across the road to the Kalaklan Bridge at Olongapo.

Demolition of the Matain and the Maquinaya bridges proved easier than the emplacement of barriers at the road that continues after Maquinaya towards the Kalaklan Bridge. For the latter mission, two big trees needed to be cut down first, and then dragged to the road that was to be obstructed, and thus effectively hold back Japanese transport vehicles and ensure meaty ambush of the occupants. Capt. Dela Paz and his men did a commendable job for the task as a whole, for when U.S. liberating forces did arrive at Subic two days later, they encountered hardly any resistance within Subic proper, and it was only in Olongapo, to which Japanese forces from all over Zambales congregated themselves, that U.S. forces met with fierce resistance that culminated in the enemy's last stand at the zigzag path between Bataan and Zambales.

Day One from American GIs' Liberation March for Subic

It was January 28, 1945. On that day—seemingly as if by sheer dictate of fate, the guerrilla brothers Eduardo and Godofredo Lesaca managed to escape from their cell at the Olongapo naval arsenal while it was being air-raided by liberating U.S. forces. After breaking in their cell's door by force, they found sheets of blankets in the building they were incarcerated in, used the sheets—in the manner of a rope—for a way out, and just let gravity pull them down to where they fell on the ground below. Everything took place as their captors were preoccupied with their own lives amid land and air attacks of the liberating forces of an enemy they had earlier humbled.

When eventually sighted by his fellow guerrillas, Capt. Lesaca looked as if he virtually was a walking corpse with wounds on his body, a broken foot, and utter haggardness resulting from a two-day ordeal of torture, starvation, and other forms of cruelty. Jose (Peping) Lesaca, Lt. Godofredo Lesaca's oldest son, who now resides in the U.S. as a retired employee of the IRS, relates, "My father, who was older than he, brought him to Bert Salang, his fellow guerrilla residing in Matain." It was there that his comrades-in-arms, right on the eve of the arrival of thousands of U.S. liberating forces, showered him with every possible life-saving first aid. In later years, he became one of the most well-known employees of the Subic Bay U.S. Naval Base, where, as one with a ranking position in the BIRO (Base Industrial Relations Office), he held the post of editor of *Subic Bay News* until he became a pensioner as a federal retiree.

7

American Liberation of Subic

American GIs who had at last freed Subiquenians from a three-year misfortune of unprecedented misery under Japan's tyrannical rule first poured ashore—without resistance—at the town of San Antonio on January 29, 1945. Only about 15 miles distant from Subic town, San Antonio is one of Zambales's coastal towns with beaches facing, at the west, the China Sea. Its strategic location was to later become a major consideration for the establishment, in its barrio San Miguel, of the U.S. Naval Communications Station at the height of the Cold (then Vietnam) War. Manned by 40,000 troops of the 38th Division and the 34th Regimental Combat Team, the San Antonio beach-landing onslaught was, incidentally, also for redemption of honor lost in defeat three years earlier in Bataan and Corregidor. It proved bloodless only because of precise planning in General Douglas MacArthur's headquarters. Intelligence operations it directed in coordination with Capt. Ramon Magsaysay's Luzon Guerrillas Command tactically served as a recipe for a well-coordinated pre-landing, anti-enemy sabotage work, that in turn, was ably executed by Capt. Jose Dela Paz Jr.'s own guerrilla command in Subic. Thus, on the very same day of the American GIs' amphibious landing at San Antonio, a motorized column subsequently advanced towards Subic—also without resistance. As it proceeded via the national road through San Marcelino and Castillejos with victory-waving GIs, townspeople, who amazedly saw for the first time "amphibious tanks" and "boat-like trucks," thickly lined the streets for welcoming that euphoria-filled Liberation Day. In Subic, horse-mounted guerrillas led a gratefully appreciative, welcoming throng, old and young, men and women. The exuberantly greeted column would soon see a series of battles that would be the prelude to the humbling, eight months later, of a once-mighty Japanese Empire into unconditional surrender to the U.S. and its allies. But what meant significantly more to Subic folks was that the liberating GIs' arrival had finally ushered in not only the relief that was so fervently craved by them from a three-year scourge of cruel Japanese rule but also a new day of hope. The fact that such a new day was to later on see most of that generation's enjoyment of life today right where their liberators had come from is simply too obvious to be argued about. By this measure, Subiquenians are thus seen to be well-blessed, and this is attributable in large measure to their hometown's being gifted by nature with a bay. Subic's geographical features have made it Zambales's first progenitor of an Olongapo City—thanks to the U.S. Navy, with the town itself now also showing signs of becoming a city—expected to be Zambales's second modern metropolis.

SIDE OPERATIONS IN SUBDUING AN ENEMY ON THE DEFENSE

Liberating Column's First Road-Fought Battle

The U.S. liberating forces' 15-mile march from San Antonio to Subic was without enemy resistance all the way only up to a little past Maquinaya, now known as Barretto, the first northern barangay portion of Olongapo bordering with Subic. It had its first battle on the way upon reaching the 50-yard Kalaklan Bridge. This bridge spans the Kalaklan River, which runs between a northern street entrance to the Olongapo Naval arsenal and the national road from Subic. The road's ending portion near the arsenal is where the Olongapo Cemetery is located. As the advancing column reached the bridge, they met their first enemy fire. It was put up partly by the Japanese soldiers who had abandoned Subic and joined with their main force in the Olongapo Naval Arsenal even prior to the San Antonio landing.

By reconnaissance, it was confirmed that billowing black smoke stemmed from the enemy's burning of things they could not save or take with them from the other side of the bridge. Also, 100-150 Japanese soldiers were seen in the bridge's Olongapo proper, committing suicide rather than face the ignominy of surrender. The liberators' superior artillery in the end made the enemy retreat and evacuate, and so the 34th Combat Team took over for taking care of later developments.

Reactivation of the Olongapo Naval Station

On January 30, 1945, just a day after their landing at San Antonio, engineers of the 38th Division immediately stationed themselves in the Olongapo Naval Arsenal for its vital reactivation. Considerable quantities of recovered lumber and other materials were used to repair bridges and buildings. Beaches and streets were cleared, and the water system was repaired.

On the same day, Grande Island, whose fuel depot and lighthouse were burned down in December 1944 via sabotage work that subsequently entailed three Hunters guerrillas' execution, was retaken. When the U.S. 5th Air Force had dropped 175 tons of bombs on the island's Fort Wint, defensive response was only light fire from a small group of Japanese anti-aircraft gunners.

Simultaneously with the retaking of the Grande Island and the reconditioning of the Olongapo Naval Base, Navy minesweepers swiftly moved to clear Subic Bay. Soon, LSTs began landing and disgorging American GIs and their equipment at Calapandayan's long beach. This was at more or less the same shore where about three years earlier, a galleon-type ship was bombed by Japanese airplanes.

Rushed Construction of Submarine Base

As reconditioning of the Subic Bay U.S. Naval Station at Olongapo went on, a separate U.S. Navy auxiliary base for its fleet of submarines started getting constructed at Agusuhin. Strategically located at an area out of an elongated, seaside portion of Subic Bay's interior that is bounded by a hugely protective mountain facing Subic town, work was rushed by a construction battalion known as Seabees. The facility is only about 2.5 miles from Subic town and the Olongapo Naval Station. Even while construction operations were going on, Subic's suitable flatlands in Calapacuan, Manggahan, and Looban became tent-studded bivouac areas, presenting a scenario of teeming GIs by the thousands in khaki and fatigue battle outfit.

Liberators' Main Battle

By the end of January 1945, it appeared that most of the Japanese forces in Zambales and its immediately adjacent province of Bataan had concentrated themselves at the rolling, hilly areas surrounding the Olongapo Zigzag Pass, which is about 3 miles from the Olongapo Naval Station. It is actually a thirty-minute winding, mountainous portion of the national road starting from Olongapo towards Bataan, Pampanga, Bulacan, and then Manila. The commander of Japanese forces in the Philippines, General Tomoyoku Yamashita, thought it tactically wise to withdraw his soldiers into defensive mountain positions, and so he ordered Colonel Sanenbou Nagayoshi to block the national highway (called Route 7) near Subic Bay. Deployed at the zigzag pass by Col. Nagayoshi were the majority of his troops, about 2,750 in all. While engineers of the 38th Division busied themselves in Subic Bay, the rest of the troops moved eastward to meet, along the zigzag pass, elements of the U.S. Army's Corps XIV that were moving westward.

As the two combined U.S. forces climbed the thick jungles of the hilly zigzag pass, they had stepped onto a veritable hornet's nest of defending Japanese, who had "honeycombed every hill and knoll with a labyrinth of 200 caves linked by tunnels."

Well-camouflaged with thick jungle foliage, their defenses were fortified with trenches and more than 70 log-and-dirt pillboxes.

This defensive tactic of the Japanese not only enabled them to delay the American advance to victory but also exacted a relatively greater per-day casualty on their attackers, compared to what occurred in Leyte. In the first three days of the zigzag fight the Americans had more casualties than during 78 days of combat in Leyte. A change in command and strategy, however, ultimately saw defeat of the Japanese. Air support by U.S. P-47 planes that carried on an intensive strafing and napalm bombing of the defenses put up by the Japanese resulted, after 15 days, in 2,400 killed among them and 25 taken as prisoners. American losses were over 1,400 killed. Subic guerrillas took part in the battle, but no casualties among them are known. "I was one of the Subic guerrillas who took part in the battle," narrates past Subic vice-mayor Augusto dela Paz.

The Olongapo Zigzag Pass Battle of '45 long remained in the memories of those who fought. This is because here and there in the sides of the hilly road—as scars of a high-mortality denouement delivered by American GIs to the enemy that had tormented them three years earlier—were left remnants of many Japanese tanks completely destroyed. Travelers in either direction on the road could hardly escape the sight.

LIBERATION'S IMMEDIATE AFTER-EFFECTS

Restored General Security in Communities

The defending Japanese forces' defeat by mid-February 1945 at the Olongapo Zigzag Pass signaled to Subic folks that the Pacific War in the Philippines was all but totally over. Actually, even prior to it, the onset of a sense of general security—mainly from the traumatic harshness of Japanese rule—pervaded practically all communities, not only in Subic but all over Zambales This was just as abruptly as sights of liberating American GIs passing by on streets in their never-before-seen types of vehicles started catching people's attention. Subicquenians' three-year life of insecurity simply dissipated as soon as the Japanese themselves disappeared and as American GIs took their place in the streets.

Liberation-Generated Jobs as a Factor in Enhancing Family Security

When full-swing work started for the reactivation of the Subic Bay Naval Station and the construction of the U.S. Navy submarine Base at Agusuhin, thousands of civilians got employed in both facilities'. Not counting Subiquenian youths who eagerly joined with the U.S. Navy, as earlier mentioned (Annex B), the number of qualified Subic workers hardly met both facilities' manpower needs, so labor was sourced from practically all of the 13 towns comprising Zambales. Many even came from other regions including—particularly in later years—Pampanga, Bataan, Tarlac, Nueva Ecija, Bicol, Mindanao, and the Visayas.

Calapandayan Becomes Subic's Busiest Barrio Next to Olongapo

Because of its long beach, Calapandayan became Subic's most LST-studded coastal barrio during the early weeks of liberation. The ships, capable of berthing on shallow water, lined Calapandayan's beach through a stretch of about half a mile. Perpendicularly positioned with their front to the beach, they were anchored about 5 meters apart from side to side. To preclude accidental harm to barrio people, Calapandayan's inhabitants living near the LSTs' berthing spots had to relocate to areas where safety was surer. The

Gonzales family, comprising the siblings Fernando, Rufina, Rosita, Pat, together with their parents was one of those whose houses were very near the ships, and so they temporarily lived in Asinan during a greater part of the liberation.

For some time, the beach became the scene of various kinds of lucrative business carried on by vendors of even bootleg liquors, "sulpak" (a kind of air-pressure hand lighter without fuel), and photos of pre-war Manila buildings, to name some typical merchandize. In the night, even some itinerant girls claiming to be Manilenas proffered "dates right on the beach" for a fee to whatever American GIs they saw around looking for a good time.

In the day, a pre-designated part of the beach was where hundreds of workers hired for work in the U.S. Navy submarine base in Agusuhin were picked by barges in the morning, then landed back in the afternoon. As many of the workers were transients and came from different towns all over Zambales, they either had to commute daily between Subic and their respective hometowns or establish board and lodging arrangements in Subic. The whole scenario thus made a boomtown out of Subic. Circulated in both U.S. currency but mostly in coins, and the Philippine peso, which commemoratively had a "VICTORY" mark on it, money flowed as never seen before. The dollar-to-peso equivalent then was 1:2, i.e., a dollar was worth two pesos.

Proliferation of Small and Big Business

Among families with limited capital, the most common kind of business they engaged in centered on snacks vending, along with what later became known as roadside sari-sari stores. Their customers were mostly workers in the U.S. submarine base in Agusuhin, and the kinds of snacks they sold—prevalently via small stores—mainly included rice cakes of assorted forms, donuts, hotcakes, coffee, and soft drinks.

One of the most successful snacks store operators of the time was run by the maternal head of a family with five children that had newly resettled their home in Subic after their evacuation months before to Wacon, Candelaria. They were in Wacon when the U.S. Liberation overtook them. The family's patriarch, who found immediate employment in the U.S. submarine base in Agusuhin, was then the schoolteacher-guerrilla who had evaded an anticipated capture after attracting the Kempetai's suspicion, in the wake of his having sent food to Balaybay farmers "zoned" and arrested as guerrilla suspects during the Japanese Occupation. The snack-store operator, who was known to most as Aling Eling, happened to have so many customers largely on account of the savory rice cakes and hotcakes she cooked that—in just less than a year—she managed to save more than a dozen gallons full of U.S. dimes and quarters as net profits after expenses, including for household needs.

Also, at practically the same time that her snack store was making good, she was able to open and run the same original grocery-clothing store that Subic's most successful Chinese businessman was to eventually own. He is Linga Young, who, as a boy of pre-war years, underwent private tutorship for basic education by Aling Eling's husband.

Linga had married a native Subicquenian, known more by most as Aling Pesiyang, and they had raised two bright children. The first, Roland C. Young, is now a successful professional doctor of medicine in California, and the second, Chit, manages their family businesses in Subic—which includes the Progress Bank.

For other families with greater capital, on the other hand, restaurants, bars, and, cabarets constituted their most common enterprises. This was then the general trend right in Subic proper, most particularly during the Liberation's early months. Although short-lived, these so-called pleasure-leisure-oriented businesses were the most lucrative in Subic at the time. There were many American GIs going around for fun, and this simply was the main contributing factor.

Profusion of Food Supply

Where hunger stalked most families almost throughout the reign in Subic of the Japanese largely because of their confiscation of crops and livestock, nourishing satiation took over during the American liberation. Food supply became abundant—in fact, this time, even of a higher-quality than before the war. Where family breadwinners happened to be employed as helpers in U.S. military installations' galleys, they were allowed to take home with them leftover but untouched food items.

"I was a helper in a field hospital in San Marcelino at the time, and the American WACs there gave us oranges or apples that were not consumed by them or others."

Such was a narration by Martin Uson, who, earlier in the Japanese Olongapo naval arsenal, had also worked as a laborer, sawing lumber.

The Birth of Subic's "Dulo"

"Dulo" is a word known to most people from or familiar with Subic as the end part of the Calapandayan road terminating at Palibunin, where the municipal cemetery is located. Since liberation, it became a byword name for Subic's red-light district, or where women plied their allure. The first brothel in it was owned and operated by a non-Subicquenian named Mamasan. For fun-seekers' health protection, those engaged in the profession routinely underwent medical check-ups—on penalty of suspension of their license in case of negative findings on their condition. Church authorities and concerned sectors of the general public all along have been against the kind of business the district has, and now it is known that what used to be the "dating" practice before is no longer existent, its prohibition being strictly enforced by the municipal government.

Arrest of Ganaps

Even as the Pacific War had not yet formally ended, all Ganaps were arrested by duly constituted authorities and thrown into prison in Manila. In a way, this was to their advantage. Relatives of guerrillas who were executed because of the Ganaps' ingratiating themselves with their Japanese masters could not but harbor deep-seated rancor against them, and their imprisonment kept them safe from people's outrage and vengeance.

But not long after Manuel A. Roxas was elected Philippine president in 1946, he granted general amnesty to all Filipinos who collaborated with the Japanese during the war. Those freed from imprisonment included all of the Ganaps in Subic.

Japanese Straggler Captured by Farmers

Four months after Subic's 1945 Liberation by American GIs, a couple of farmers in Mapanao chanced upon a lone Japanese soldier who was obviously hiding in the barrio's thick woodlands. Still in a uniform that was totally in a tattered condition, the straggler was hogtied and carried, on a pole on his captors' shoulders, in the manner of a pig being delivered to the butcher's house, to Subic's municipal building. "There, the incumbent Mayor, Leopoldo Lauzares, good-heartedly relieved the prisoner's discomfort by according him proper physical handling and arranging for his immediate turn over to American authorities," relates Maxima D. Tala, who added that at the time, Captain Ramon Magsaysay was one of Mayor Lauzares' frequent visitors.

Patriarch of Prominent Family Commits Suicide

It was a most startling piece of news to most of Subic folks when they woke up one morning unexpectedly hearing that Jose dela Paz, Sr., father of Subic's foremost guerrilla hero, Captain Peping dela Paz, Jr., had slit his own throat. His motivation remains unsure, but continues to spark curiosity to this day. More popularly known as Mang Pepe, his blood-soaked body was found lifeless in the "aplaya" or the seashore near his family's house that has remained at exactly the same spot it was at before the war. The area is adjacently to the left or east of the roadside spot where passers-by had to bow to the Japanese soldier in the sentry shed during the war.

Onset of Maquinaya NSD Pilferage-Based Buy-and-Sell Business

For some months following liberation, Maquinaya, more popularly known now as Barretto, was where the biggest depot for U.S. surplus military vehicles, equipment, and spare part was located. Jeeps, weapons carriers, six-by-six trucks, tires, etc. were kept in the depot. It became known as the NSD (Naval Supply Depot), and its location, which was just beside a national road and not inside the Olongapo naval station where security was relatively stricter, predisposed it to on-and-off pilferage. Only when some men got killed while in the act of stealing spare parts for a lucrative buy-and-sell business, did pilferage in the depot come to a complete stop.

Emergence of Jeepneys: Common People's Transport Vehicle

If there is any particular "commute vehicle" that was sort of invented soon after liberation, purely as a result of Filipino ingenuity, that led to the first-time emergence of cheap mass transit under Philippine standards, it is the "jeepney." In Subic, vehicles of the jeep type that were used by liberating American GIs so abounded as surplus after Japan's surrender in September 1945 that entrepreneurs saw suitable use for them. The military-olive-green, two-seat vehicle was renovated into the multicolored/decorated ten-seat design now commonly seen in virtually every nook and corner of the Philippines.

As means of earning a living, the "jeepney"—as the "invention" is now called, proved very significant in enabling many an average family to support the education of their children.

Birth of Electric Power

Shortly after liberation, electricity became available in Subic for the first time. But it was only for lighting homes at the most—with supply made commercially available only at night. A diesel-fed generator acquired as a U.S. Navy property surplus by Vicente Nepomuceno, a businessman in Ilwas, powered the town's early energy needs. It served many families for years, and only after a bigger electric plant was put up in Calapandayan did it go out of business.

Birth of First High School in Subic

Subic's first high school was established in about mid-1945. Its main building was the Saint James Hall of the Subic Parish Church, so it became officially known as the Saint James High School. Its first principal was Mr. Blanco. At the time, Subic's peace-and-order conditions were sort of unstable. This was because "Huks"—a term applied originally to the ideological followers of their Supremo Luis Taruc but later partly metamorphosed into plain bandits—were said to have established a foothold in town. This was because Subic then was a booming town, thanks to the Olongapo Naval Station's reactivation and the Agusuhin USN submarine base's operations.

The degree of Subic's peace-and-order instability attributed to fear of the "Huks" at the time is somehow reflected in a school deployment incident. Located near the Subic Catholic Church and the Subic Municipal Hall, the school had then only about 50 students. Suddenly, while classes were on, sounds of rapid gunfire reverberated within and outside the school building! The principal, apprehensively thinking that "Huks" were on an attacking spree, yelled to all students, "Deploy, deploy!"

Students did deploy but their act and Mr. Blanco's cautioning yells were unnecessary. One discipline-short student had played a prank, as he was wont to, and this time what he stealthily did was to set firecrackers on fire in an unknown place in the school. Because of the incident and because he failed to learn who the prankster was, the principal served only for one year in the school.

Attention-Robbing Student's Prank in High School Drama

In 1947, the Saint James High School had an algebra teacher who also taught English literature, a subject she well handled partly via the staging of dramatic plays. She was Mrs. Perla Reyes, who earned renown as one of the school's good teachers—but most particularly for the stage plays she had planned and directed, with selected students as "budding actresses and actors." Apparently because of the limelight afforded most, if not all, of the talented participants in her widely acclaimed staged dramas, an unduly ambitious student once played a self-serving prank on a fellow student, who happened to have a stellar role in a certain play scheduled for soldiers' entertainment in San Marcelino. On the night of the play, while aboard a truck on the way to San Marcelino from Subic, the schemer tempted discipline-short classmates into making his quarry get drunk. Then he presented himself as a ready, on-the-spot substitute actor for the night's drama. The prankster did succeed in taking the part and acting in the place of the (victimized) student he had trickily made "unavailable"—but proved that he had anything but a worthy mettle of intellect.

8

Post-Liberation Period

The liberation euphoria in Subic lasted until Japan's formal surrender to General Douglas MacArthur in September 1945. With the Pacific War then already ended, American GIs, except those stationed as regulars in the reconditioned Olongapo naval Base, had left Subic for their trip back home in the U.S. Also, the U.S. Navy submarine base at Agusuhin was made defunct, along with the abandonment in Subic Bay of some LSTs seen as no longer operational. Other war materials deemed dispensable included a heap of unused bullets of assorted calibers that were piled up about nine cubic meters in volume near the Subic Bridge. Mainly because of the war's end, practically all kinds of businesses just suddenly waned in their moneymaking capacities. But this was not the case in Subic's then barrio of Olongapo where, by virtue of its being the locale of the U.S. Naval station, the entity's operations continued to prop up what was a military-based economy. The Cold War that started soon after World War II made it imperative for the mutual national interests of both the U.S. and the Philippines that the Olongapo Naval Arsenal be maintained. It was thus that even after Philippine Independence on July 4, 1946, the Military Bases Agreement was signed in March 1947. It provided for a 99-year lease and control by the U.S. of twenty-three military installations in the Philippines, including the extensive Subic Bay Naval Facilities and the Clark Airbase. In the Subic Bay U.S. Naval Facility complex alone, more than 15,000 civilian workers got employed for years until the U.S. Navy pullout in the early 2000s.

MAJOR EVENTS IN THE WAKE OF JAPAN'S SURRENDER

Discontinued Operation of the Subic Bay U.S. Submarine Base

The new submarine base speedily constructed at Agusuhin by U.S. Navy Seabees in the course of Subic's liberation in January 1945 ceased operating within less than a year of the liberating GIs' stay in Subic. It, in fact, got phased out shortly after Japan's formal acceptance of defeat from the U.S. some eight months later, or in September 1945. One inevitable result was also the phasing out of most of the leisure-oriented lines of business in Subic proper. Also, many civilians were laid off from their jobs in the base. But there were those who got reemployed later in other U.S. military installations not only in the Philippines but also in places outside of it—like Guam, Okinawa, and Saipan. In the Philippines, the biggest U.S. military installation that remained the biggest employer was the U.S. Naval Station at Olongapo. In fact, even in later years, it continued to be the induction center also for young men not only from Subic but throughout the country who desired to join with the U.S. Navy.

Upon abandonment of the Agusuhin submarine base, its structures and facilities that could not be saved were all practically left to people who were the first to gain access to them. Plywood, assorted pieces of reusable lumber, roofing sheets, electric cable, ice-making machines, plumbing materials, etc., etc., typified various kinds of worthy materials that many Subic folks had benefited themselves with.

"Five-Six" at Its Peak

Used as a "loan-sharking" term, "five-six" is referred to in Subic as a money lender's practice of personally loaning out money to borrowers at an interest rate of 240% per annum. This sounds excessive as compared to ordinary rates of, say, 10% per year, but it has stayed on to this day. How great the difference is shown by this simple illustration. When an amount of money borrowed is, say, P50.00, repayment to the lender is automatically P60.00, after just a period of one month. The cost of the loan is thus P10.00 per month, to wit: P60.00 - P50.00 = P10.00. On a per-year basis, by which cost of borrowed money is ordinarily computed as allowed by law, this loan cost of P10.00 for the P50.00-principal amount borrowed cumulatively builds up to P120.00 in a year, and this equivalently rates 240% as interest per year, figured thus: P120.00 interest per year divided by (P50.00 principal or amount of loan) x 100 = 240%.

From this, one can easily see that a money borrower is loaned out P500.00, the lender enjoys a profit from the former of P1,200.00, computed thus: P500.00 x 240% = P500.00 x 2.4 = P1, 200.00—instead of supposedly just some P50.00 under the exampled 10% ordinary interest rate—as figured thus: P500.00 x 10% = P500.00 x 1 = P50.00.

As banking began operating in Subic only in the 1970s, loan-sharking, which reached its peak not long after the National Independence of 1946, had enabled many of the town's shrewd business enterprisers to prosper over others' financial inadequacy. Most of them have already gone, but new ones have taken their place in the town's scene of personal money lending for profit.

Unsolved Murder in Matain

One murder case in Subic that to this day remains unsolved as to perpetrator and motive took place in Matain in the 1950s. The incident became a much-talked about tragedy, largely because of the victim's being a patriarch of the barrio's famous De Perio family. In fact, he once served as pre-war Subic mayor. It was partly for the family's popularity that two other De Perios, both sons of the murdered elder De Perio, also became political stalwarts in Subic. One similarly served as Subic mayor; the other, who was younger, Olongapo vice-mayor—and, as a stellar baseball player through many years, was more popularly known as "Junior."

"Jueting" Enjoys an Enduring Heyday

Although it was already in existence in Subic even during the pre-war, "jueting" heightened up to "variably two games a day" within the 1946-1990 period. A migrant family from Cavite was popularly known to have profited well as the sole direct operator of the game within the period. So much fuss of unprecedented, national scope and controversy has spewed out of it in variously associated, unresolved issues, but the fact that it has proven to be an oasis of livelihood among many job part-timers or full-timers could hardly be denied or discounted. In many openly known cases, not few families are known to have succeeded in making both ends meet only because of their breadwinners' having served as regular "cobradors" (or bet collectors).

Diesel Spill Benefits the Idle

When some run-down LSTs were left in Subic Bay after liberation, in a part of the sea fronting the Wawandue barrio, they just happened to entirely spill their content of diesel fuel. The strongly kerosene-scented fluid was of such voluminous quantity that its thickness ranged from 3-4 inches as it floated and flowed with the waves toward mainly the Wawandue shoreline (filled in with earth in later years to accommodate a relocated, new public market and other permanent public buildings near it).

For a tempting price offer by a local businessman, the thickly collecting oil at Wawandue's shore disappeared in just about two days. People who had no work to do and wanted easy money flocked individually or in groups to the shoreline, scooped the wasted oil with cups, and saved it into drums and other receptacles they could take hold of. They got paid cash for the task, and the businessman made some profit out of the spilled oil.

Fun and Money Derived from Unused Bullets

For some months, in a part of the Calapandayan beach just a stone's-throw away from the foot of the Subic Bridge, a heap of unused bullets of different calibers piled up to a volume of about nine cubic meters hardly escaped the attention of passers-by. All the bullets were not contained in cartridges, but were loose. The war's having just ended then at the time was thought simply to be the reason for the ammunition's being just left to the mercy of the elements. But to young boys who now and then used the railing of the bridge as a diving board for bathing in the water below it, the bullets—particularly the .52-caliber ones—served as a source of underwater lighting spectacle, which even onlookers momentarily enjoyed. When a bullet's lead is removed, the remaining powder in the capsule is set on fire, and the whole seething thing is thrown into the water below the bridge. Even if under water, the "fired" capsule continues to burn for some time, and the bright illumination generated in the water is what fascinates onlookers.

On the main, however, the wasted ammunition ended up with wiser use in the hands of metal scrap gatherers and dealers. It remained unknown, though, how much money they acquired from the discarded bullets, expending only their time and effort.

Subic Becomes a Melting Pot

Mainly because of the broad spectrum of jobs and business opportunities engendered by the short or long-term operations of the U.S. military installations in Subic on its liberation and then after Japan's surrender, the town metamorphosed almost overnight—so to speak—into a melting pot! Where its pre-liberation population was composed mainly of Tagalogs and some Ilocanos, what had been, for three years, a struggling, enemy-shackled town that agonizingly braved pangs of hunger and disease became transformed. General Douglas MacArthur's much-awaited return reinvigorated Subic—and certainly other towns—into a community more vibrant than before, that was replete with an unprecedented admixture of various ethnic groups of different origins: Kapampangan, Zambale, Caviteno, Batangueno, Bicolano, Bisaya, Waray, Moro, etc., etc. Many of them became either business owners in Subic and Olongapo, workers in both public and private entities including U.S. military facilities/installations, or inductees into the U.S. Navy. And most, if not all, of them now are known to be residing in the U.S. as naturalized citizens.

POST-INDEPENDENCE EVENTS OF FAR-REACHING SIGNIFICANCE

The Philippine Constabulary Preserves Peace and Order in Subic

Shortly after liberation and proclamation of Philippine independence on July 4, 1947, Subic was one of many towns in the Philippines where the Philippine Constabulary as the country's national police, had put a detachment of its forces to preserve peace and order.

At the time, the Huks, who were then strongly anti-Japanese, found themselves outlawed by the new independent Philippine government for their post-liberation activities. While their grievances were fundamentally agrarian in nature and concerned more with unresolved economic squabbles with their landlords, their ideological pursuits were seen to run counter to government's interests; hence they continued to be perceived to be a pernicious threat to society. To thus forestall perpetration by them of subversive activities in Subic, where money flow became easier by virtue of the proliferation of multi-natured businesses in it, maintenance of a Subic Philippine Constabulary command was deemed essential. It was maintained even up to the Martial Law years.

Military Bases Agreement

On March 14, 1947, The US-RP Military Bases Agreement was mutually approved. It stipulated U.S. control of the Subic Bay U.S. Naval Base, among other U.S. military installations in the Philippines. It also provided for retention of Subic's barrio Olongapo under the administration of the U.S. Naval Reservation. Under this setup, the naval base commanding officer remained serving as chairman also of the Olongapo council, the school board, the hospital board, and other governing agencies.

On 1951, the heightening of the Cold War necessitated construction of the Cubi Point, a defensive war infrastructure complex, entailing work almost equivalent to the magnitude of that undertaken for the Panama Canal. The U.S. Navy Seabees were tasked for it, with the Pomeroy-Hawaiian Dredging Bechtel Company, Inc., serving as private contractor. Thousands of Filipinos hired during project construction came from almost all of the eight regions of the Philippines.

Olongapo Gets Inundated with Deforestation-Caused Rainwater

In 1955, Olongapo got entirely flooded—for the first time since time immemorial—with up to breast-high rainwater. At the time, the population, particularly of Olongapo, had built up fast. In establishing their homes in the Olongapo Zigsag Pass, where years before Japanese soldiers on the run had virtually made a Custer's-last-stand type defense, people wantonly cleared forest areas for building their houses. Collectively, the practice resulted in fast run-off in hilly areas during the rainy days, thereby giving rise to an unprecedented flooding. It lasted only less than a day and caused no loss of life or property

Administrative Control of Olongapo Relinquished to Philippine Government

Because of the seemingly odd scenario of a supposedly independent population of 60,000 Filipinos' remaining under the administrative control of a U.S. base commander of a military installation over which he naturally had an overall sway, the Military Bases Agreement was amended on December 7, 1959. By it, the U.S. relinquished control of Olongapo to the Philippine government. Included in the turnover were all water, telephone, and electrical facilities, collectively worth about $6 million.

Olongapo Becomes a City—and Sees Assassination of Its First Mayor

Not long after its local administration was turned over by the U.S. to the Philippine government in 1959, Olongapo converted into a city. Its sizable income and population were principal factors that accounted for the change. As a city, its first elected mayor was Jimmy Gordon, father of incumbent Philippine Senator Richard J. Gordon. The new mayor was murdered at the lobby near stairway to his office at the Olongapo City Hall, and the incident was the first of its kind to occur in Zambales. Olongapo greatly mourned the mayor's death, because it happened at the height of his services to the general public. Their sentiment in this regard was what eventually made him looked up to as the "Father of Olongapo City." The gunman was apprehended, and the identities of the duo that instigated the crime were learned. But what was thought to be the right solution to the problem was for the bullet-felled mayor's spouse, herself, to keep up the fight right in Olongapo's political arena. And so, by the people's mandate in a subsequent mayoral election, Amelia J. Gordon saw herself elected, seemingly by fate's dictate for her to continue the work begun by her murdered husband.

Money Flow Heightens in Subic

If there was any aspect of the Cold War that put a heavy workload on the Subic Bay U.S. Naval Base's operations, it was the Vietnam War. From 1964 to 1968, about 98 to 215 ships per month were served in the base for repair, supply delivery/replenishment, etc. Prior to the period, the number of ships anchored at the facility for generally similar purposes averaged only 30.

To Subic's and particularly Olongapo City's own economy, the magnitude of ship traffic meant much flow of money. This is especially so if even just one aircraft carrier berthed at the base. An aircraft carrier has a crew of up to 5,000, and from this number alone can be easily imagined how much money sailors spend for personal fun outside the base as they take time off their daily chores at the seas.

Actually, every time an aircraft carrier or another other large ship anchored at Subic Bay, the event always sort of presaged to most enterprising people the flow of some money into the streets. It was simply like a fiesta, where there is much rejoicing in all places, but not because of certain special cultural or traditional spectacles to behold but money that palpably flows bountifully around—to shops, passenger drivers, bargirls, restaurants, and other business instrumentalities—out of U.S. sailors having a good time in their favorite places of fun.

In Subic's "Dulo" and in other similar places in Olongapo City, everyone became highly spirited with sweet smiles on their faces every time throngs of sailors emerged in the streets for search of exotic fun.

Masinlocqueno Finds Jobs for Many

Many supervisory jobs in the Subic U.S. Naval Base were held by Subicquenians. But at the height of the Vietnam War in the 1960s, during which job opportunities increased in the base, particularly in its Navy Exchange, which served aggregately about 4,225,000 servicemen for exchange transactions that involved a total of some $25 million from 1964 through 1968 alone, it took not a Subicquenian but a Masinlocquenio who had married one from Subic to be instrumental in the employment of the highest number of Subic residents in the department and other sectors of the base.

He is known more by the name of Mang Pendong Egana. He relocated to Subic from his hometown of Masinloc, the second-to-the-last northern town of Sta. Cruz, Zambales, when job vacancies arose in the U.S. Naval Base in Olongapo starting in 1960. Already deceased due to cancer, to which he succumbed in Manila in 2005, he is survived by his widow, Mrs. Leonila D. Egana, and their children, all of whom are now in the U.S.

Cars, a Luxury and Symbol of Status

The common man's kind of personal transport vehicle in Subic or most anywhere else in the Philippines is the jeep—either passenger-converted or for-family-use type. It is a sort of necessity among most families. But among the more moneyed, cars were seen to be more of a luxury. In Subic, Jose De La Paz, Jr. and Luis Afable were the first to own family cars.

They had received much back pay as guerrillas, and they had wisely engaged in lucrative business not long after the liberation. De La Paz embarked on agricultural machinery service, ranching business, and a logging enterprise.

Lucrative Business out of U.S. Military Surplus Trucks

Where the four-seat jeep of the U.S. Army found a very useful purpose at war's end by being renovated into a 10-seat passenger vehicle, its weapons carrier and six-by-six truck ended up—out of surplus—as multi-purpose transport units used profitably in many rural and urban homes. In barrios, the weapons carrier commonly became used for hauling farm products to market, as well as for threshing rice out of its stalks after harvest. Among rice dealers, it was used to transport rice supply contained in individual sacks from rice mills to individual households for pre-contracted monthly sale. For some years, the sturdy, all-weather vehicle greatly facilitated transportation of merchandize from almost any source to the market.

On the other hand, the six-by-six truck became a standard hauling vehicle among loggers. Its power takeoff proved quite handy as a labor-saving or job-simplifying device.

As a six wheeler, it proved just rightly powerful, too, even in muddy and steeply graded roads. And where regular passenger or commodity liners had not yet come into operation, the truck remained for sometime a sort of a commercial transport vehicle.

Rise in Cigarette Smuggling

For purposes of evading tax, U.S.-brand cigarettes—Camel, Lucky Strike, Chesterfield, Salem, Union, Philip Morris, etc.—had for years become a very lucrative commodity for in-bound smuggling. Although commercially priced at more than twice the cost of local brands, the commodity's flavor held such sway over smokers that they dido not care much about the extra cost entailed for access to the good-tasting but addictive contraband.

It is thus that for easy, big money, in-bound cigarette smuggling—most often from Honkong—had lured even high-placed political leaders. But while the under-the-table practice did sustain the audacious for holding a desired political power that became always possible only under possession of much money, it nevertheless did not endure favorably with time. Dishonor and maimed reputation inevitably took over what was originally passed off as integrity.

Subic was often a landing spot for smuggled cigarettes, with use of fuel tankers as transport vehicle. That the illegal activity goes on despite existing laws against it is a matter that does not escape the notice of the general public in Subic. Thus, when once a candidate for reelection as provincial governor was mentioned in political campaigns as being indiscreetly involved, the outcome readily saw a budding, neophyte political leader, Vicente (Vic) Magsaysay, the people's winning choice.

First Mini-Subdivision Project

The project was called the "dela Paz compound." It was not a large-scale subdivision complete with interlinking roads and other facilities needed to take care of occupants' service needs, but it nonetheless matched families' preferences for renting homes instead of individually owning. Established in the 1950s in Calapacuan, it was owned and operated by Angel dela Paz, a Subiquenian who happened to occupy a high executive position in the Development Bank of the Philippines. The project consisted of fewer than ten home units, but it illustrated how the right exercise of influence and connections could help contribute to a community's socio-economic progress.

Reclusive Subiquenian Pensioner Murdered

An original Subiquenian who spent most of his years working in the U.S. until his retirement in the 1960s, came back to Subic and established his supposedly permanent home in a once-swampy land in Camachile. He was a sibling of Mang Pepe dela Paz, and he chose to live alone by himself—i.e., without even so much as a helper in his past-middle-age remaining years. As he received a retirement pension in dollars, it became to be known that he was "moneyed." This, plus the fact that he chose a reclusive way of living, was deemed the reason for his having become a victim of murder right in his companionless Camachile home. But to this day whatever was really the motivation behind his murder remains a matter of pure speculation, for no one was ever pinpointed as the tragedy's perpetrator.

Gigantic Mudslide in Palibunin

In 1979, an unprecedented mudslide occurred in the ending part of Subic's "Dulo"—at a sizable portion of the mountain called Palibunin. It resulted in severe transportation dislocations for days, death to one person buried alive, and injuries to several passengers of a vehicle that was hit by earth debris cascading from a hilltop down to the road below.

The catastrophe was ascribed to heavy rains—but this was not the true cause. Occurrence of heavy rains each year is not unusual in Subic since time immemorial. But the town's 1979 first-time mudslide—or any others after it—actually resulted from the adverse effect of indiscriminate practice of "kaingin" (a crude process of vegetation burning preceded planting of crops), as well as of denuding tops and sides of mountains unwisely earmarked for subdivision projects.

In terms of overall costs—such as for clearing and for concrete works needed for repair or cave-in preventive rip-raping, the Subic Municipal Treasury naturally appeared drained of an otherwise unnecessary expenditure for the Palibunin mudslide. This is veritably an administrative folly.

To enlightened environmentalists, deforestation is known to adversely predispose mountains to the erosive effects of surface runoff—the flow of rainwater in any place of higher-to-lower elevation. Trees, bushes, and grasses as natural protective clothing of the earth significantly help prevent soil erosion. Their root network holds soil in place, while their fallen foliage not only absorbs water but also slows down its flow, thereby helping curb erosion—which tends to speed up with rain where soil is bare of protective covering. But it seems this matter was beyond administrative concerns in the granting of a statutory permit for subdivision developers in Subic at the time.

Most people are not aware of it, but ancient history shows that the whole Sahara has not always been the extensive desert that it is today, but partly was once alive with lush vegetation. But indiscriminate logging to build ships vital to the making of the Roman Empire was carried out to such extent that what were once large tracts of richly forested lands were converted into parched, barren areas until they eventually evolved into dry, desert lands—thanks to wind-caused erosion, as well.

That the recurrences of mudslides happen only usually where and when indiscreet deforestation and other ways of denuding mountains are done, shows and supports this argument about erosion.

Mount Pinatubo Erupts After 500 Years

Mt. Pinatubo is a mountainous part of a chain of volcanoes bordering the western side of Luzon. Located at the central portion of the Zambales Range, it stands 1,745 meters high above sea level and is visible at the horizon from any vicinity in Luzon where one's view remains plainly unobstructed. After exploding once on June 9 and three times on June 12, 1991, its height ebbed down 300 meters; it became almost 20% lower—the result of the lopping off a part of it by its own explosion.

Mt. Pinatubo's eruption caught worldwide attention because of the global extent to which its volcanic ash had flown with the atmosphere's ocean of air. Volcanic clouds reached and spread out 25,000 meters high above the horizon in practically every part of the globe for days.

When on June 15, 1991, a storm passed by the volcano that had been awakened from a 500-year slumber, rain, thunder, lightning, and earthquakes interspersed with ash floating in the atmosphere, with the resultant mud-dense downpour, caused roofs of many buildings to collapse. Dry ash also rendered many airplanes, particularly in the Clark Airbase that is within the neighborhood of the exploding volcano, inoperable for some time.

Daytime suddenly turned into a night-like darkness that pervaded all over Subic, Olongapo, Castillejos, and San Marcelino. People, some of whom speculated a "coming of the end of the world," evacuated to other seemingly unaffected places. They walked through inter-town distances, what with road transportation having stopped, due to impassable, muddy or volcanic ash-filled streets.

Damage to infrastructure and property was estimated to have reached hundreds of millions of dollars. Human casualties were recorded as 867 dead, 184 injured, and 23 missing. Residential dislocations also followed, with many families permanently allocated new land spaces to rebuild their life and homes. Being mostly residents of the Zambales Range, Aetas, as the most affected, comprised 94% of evacuees to relocation centers.

Purely Faith-Based Reliance for Help Among Mt. Pinatubo Eruption's Victims

The Carmelite Monastery of the Holy Spirit at Subic's barrio, Ilwas, was one of the most substantially damaged buildings in the town during the Mt.

Pinatubo explosion '91. Donations by many of Subic's faithful, both local and abroad, particularly in the U.S., had done much in the monastery chapel's reconditioning. But edifice's aging gave rise to the need for an entirely new and larger chapel.

As the Carmelite entity's nuns did not have the resources for this huge undertaking, except solely Divine Providence's graces, they could not but confidently look up to all the faithful of Jesus Christ's human flock for realizing their hope for a new house of worship, in the practice of their religious, contemplative life—during which many of the laity participate when any Mass is held in the chapel. The founding of the Carmelite Monastery in Subic was spearheaded by Mother Natividad Dison. It is now headed by Sr. Amparo in her capacity as prioress of the Subic Carmel of the Holy Spirit, OCD. Sr. Mary Albina serves in an assisting capacity. Currently serving as the monastery chaplain is Father Edwin B. Mertola, who hails from Sta. Cruz, Zambales.

Plan for 10-Year Extended Stay of U.S. Navy in Subic Quashed

On August 1991, U.S. and Philippine negotiators had come up with a plan to extend by 10 years the expiring Military Bases Agreement in return for a $360-million payment to the Philippine government for the first year and $203 million for the remaining nine years.

But not all of the Filipino political leaders were in favor, despite a strongly favoring stand of most Filipinos, particularly those connected, directly or indirectly, with the Subic Bay Naval Base and other U.S. military installations in the Philippines.

Thus, with the eruption of Mt. Pinatubo, that more or less coincided with the waning of the Cold War at the time, all U.S. military facilities, which could only entail huge budgets to maintain, were left by the American forces.

But all the facilities and infrastructure they left somehow compensatively seeded what has since sprouted into what is now the Subic Bay Metropolitan Development Authority, a major generator of economic power being harnessed for all its benefits at the national, provincial, and local levels of government.

9

Subiquenians' Emigration to the U.S.

Regardless of Subiquenians who had joined with the U.S. Navy and subsequently brought along with them their qualified relatives to the U.S., countless Subic Bay Naval Base workers had rendered creditable service. As a result, they earned special immigrant visas. By this, most of them had thus decided to emigrate—and metamorphosed into permanent expatriates in the U.S. The emigration of Subiquenians, particularly those who became connected with the U.S Navy or the Subic Bay U.S. Naval Base, directly or indirectly, actually started even during the early part of the post-liberation period. It gained momentum over the years, and this was particularly so not long after the U.S. Navy pulled out of Subic. Among the great majority of emigrants, relatively higher standard of living, better opportunities not ordinarily available elsewhere, high-quality health care, higher levels and broader ranges of social security, cleaner air and other components of the environment, and other factors not obtaining in the Philippines count as the main motivating factors. The fact that very few of them, if any, have decided on resettling back to their past hometown is inarguably supportive of this fact.

SUBICQUENIANS IN PEDESTALS OF ILLUSTRIOUSNESS IN THE U.S.

If attainment of a relatively higher level of living is a measure itself of success, then all Subiquenian immigrants or any others who had earned naturalization into American citizenship could be seen successful, indeed.

But it is an incontrovertible truism that—as most people see—success comes in varying forms, nature, and significance. Nothing is deemed as having more impact on others or society itself than when someone becomes an illustrious role model whose achievements are worth emulating by any society's succeeding generations.

In the U.S., there are today many successful Subiquenians looked up by virtue of the nature of their chosen professions. They belong to the particular kind of professionals commonly identified with the rise of "brain drain," not necessarily from Subic alone but the Philippines as a whole. Many of these are doctors of medicine, a skill field of high-income, especially in the U.S. Subiquenian doctors doing quite well in America in this regard are known to include Doctors Angel Milliora, Eduardo S. Ornedo, Lenny De La Paz, and Samuel Reyes.

On the other hand, there are also Subiquenians whose reputable professions alone were not solely instrumental for their being held in as much esteem by their peers. Instead, it is their own inherent assets of personal integrity, patience, and steadfastness in the face of life's myriad trying challenges.

The from-Rags-to-Riches Girl

Formerly only a poor salesgirl in an ordinary metallic gadgetry bazaar in Manila, Milna dela Paz, who had the misfortune of having been paternally neglected—in fact, even completely abandoned while in adolescence, is now a big-time owner-manager of four franchised restaurants (after selling one) in the U.S. As the second of the four children of Rosalina V. Natividad, by her common-law husband who denied her all through their conjugal life—the benefit of not only matrimony but also voluntary spousal support, Milna struggled hard in her way through Subic's St. James High School, then the University of the Philippines for a degree in business.

Under the family situation she was faced with out of her father's unfulfilled bounden duty as supposedly a responsible-minded parent, only her relatives' help and her own mother's meager income as a small dress shop owner-worker did the rest in sustaining her needs. But what counted most in this regard was her own determination to overcome obstacles in her way—as aided in the process with her mother's faithful character, partly molded during her pre-war dressmaking-training stint at the Immaculate Conception Seminary in Manila.

As is the case with many Subicquenian ladies at the time, Milna got married to a U.S. Navy Filipino sailor, Raul Espiritu. It was then that she became an immigrant to the U.S. But for reasons only known to themselves as couples, they had parted ways, accordingly observing what law provides.

Presently, she is now known as Mrs. Milna De la Paz Freedman, and this is by virtue of her having re-entered marital life—with an American computer engineer. As a voluntary civic activity, she serves as treasurer of the Subic Association of San Diego, California, where she lives. Relatives have nothing in themselves but hope that she remains successful and worth being emulated in all respects by others.

From Sacristan to Businessman

Manuel Israel, a Bicolano by ethnicity, used to be known in Subic as the town's Catholic Church sacristan in his adolescence, working his way through the St. James High School. Employed after graduation at the Subic Bay U.S. Naval Base in Olongapo, he was one of many who had rendered creditable service. So, like countless others, he qualified for a special immigrant visa for entry to the U.S. And when the U.S. navy pulled out from Subic in the 1990s, he used his visa for emigration from the town, bringing along his wife, the former Mila A. Custodio, and their two teen-aged children shortly thereafter.

Now, in the course of only some fifteen years, a period generally equivalent to the waiting time for statutory grant of naturalized citizens' petition for their relatives' immigration also into the U.S., Manuel had managed to already own two houses in Las Vegas—with one for rent. Besides he also had put up a family business managed jointly by his two sons, Julius and JG.

If his achievement of this nature and extent is seen to sort of assume a milestone of significance, it is simply because of his start from nothing more than a humble church's aide. But beyond this, his success directly stems from the fact that the very same job skills—in structural materials, welds, and various aspects of engineering works—that he had cumulatively gained mastery of as a Subic Bay U.S. Naval Base employee are what he happened to embark on since his migration to the U.S. with his family.

Humble Barrio Lass-Turned Medical Doctor Via Magna Cum Laude Scholarship

Born into but an ordinary family, Erlita P. Gadin was still in her teens when her parents, Ernesto and Orlita P. Gadin, respectively a past worker at the Subic Bay U.S. Naval Base and an ex-employee of the Olongapo General Hospital, immigrated to the U.S. in the 1980s. While in college in San Antonio, Texas, she became paternally orphaned as a result of her father's untimely death from a vehicular accident. But this did not deter her from pursuing her ambition to be a doctor of medicine. When she graduated with the rank of magna cum laude from college, a statutory financial assistance she applied for enabled her to further her studies until realizing a doctorate degree in medicine. Without her exemplary academic performance, she never would have achieved her ambition, what with her family's financial limitations! She is now doing quite well professionally as a hospital pediatrician in Philadelphia.

From Bamban to Subic Once, Then to Big-Time Business Partner Now

In her adolescence during the late 1980s, Analy (Lyn) Manalo migrated to Subic without permanently abandoning her original home at Bamban, Tarlac. As if by fate, Derick Lee Drumm, an American sailor from the U.S. Navy, who interchangeably spent time in 1988-1990 between the Clark Airbase at Pampanga and the Subic Bay U.S. Naval Base, happened to know her. Cupid's arrow afterwards apparently struck both—with the eventual result of Lyn's being seen as now one of the few most successful U.S. Navy brides simultaneously serving in the capacity of both a running a household and being a business partner. Not long after her arrival in 1991 at the U.S. on the strength of Derick's fiancée petition for her, she found it worthwhile to engage in self-employment, as she needed to take care of their home and children. With nothing more than pen and notebook plus sheer determination, she decided to take special school courses, and this culminated into her now running of their family-owned Drumm Insurance Services at Union City, California—in her capacity as a licensed broker. In addition, she serves with her husband as joint realtors for California's Keller Williams Benchmark Properties. In addition to this she gets satisfaction from civic pursuits. She finds time to head, as president, the Bambanese Association USA of Nor-Cal. Typically, Lyn exemplifies how any others of ordinary beginnings could be atop the crest of success commonly associated with the myriad opportunities of the American dream.

10

Particularly Notable Subiquenians

In Subic over the years, many persons are known to have gained some fame or renown. Most of them became prominent because of their success in their callings, attainment of high positions in government or private entities, etc. But to most people, this does not totally and necessarily mean exemplary illustriousness, a personal quality tending to make for enduring memories generally beneficial to succeeding generations or posterity itself. If this is seen so, it is because most know that even mere personal and family relations could easily be a major influencing or determinant factor in fostering connections for one's carving or landing of famous positions in the socio-economic structure of society. Another known reason stems from their cognizance of the fact that just as a book's content cannot be judged by its cover, so also is it true to them that anyone's notability rests not with its outer coatings but more with an inner sterling character. Subic abounds with citizens short of professional or material renown and prominence—as otherwise usually associated only, partly or wholly, with high-level placements or impressiveness of material possessions—which in the town are seen to come ordinarily in the form of particularly affluent-looking and stylish residential houses or other luxurious kinds of property owned—like jewelry, business establishments put up or run, or personal or family vehicles used. But their examples and established ways of day-to-day living as peace-loving and law-abiding members of the Subic community are such that most of them could only be looked up to as somehow worth emulating by the less lucky of their peers or by just the normally ambitious or principle-minded others. Made up of an admixture of professionals and just ordinary, average-means citizens, they are or were engaged in occupational pursuits that are as varied as life's myriad opportunities. But they all appear to be inherently possessed of virtues valued in the realm of public or private life or service: unpretentiously altruistic ways or palpably innate humanness and unassuming practice of people-to-people dealings that make anyone feel always trustful of, friendly, or comfortable with them. In another vein, they exemplify those whom parents would unabashedly be glad to point out—for desired upbringing outcomes—as examples to their children, and this is all because of their golden character that distinguishes them. There are a plethora Subiquenians definitely known to belong to this prominence category, and the circumstances of the most notable of them are here described briefly—in alphabetical order by family name.

Nicolas "Lipac-Lipac" Cleto Adolfo—A poor Calapacuan as a youth, he worked his way through college to become a lawyer. Sheer keenness of mind about law plus his "common man's ways" drew unsurpassed number of clients to him, as a result of which he became nicknamed "Lipac-Lipac"—meaning "lots of money." A heart attack downed him during his incumbency as Subic judge.

Alfredo Afable—Looking like a business tycoon, but being soft-spoken, he was fondly known more as a neighborhood friend, Peding. His outgoing, casual ways with people, old and young alike, endeared him to them to such extent that he easily became a Subic mayor. His incumbency was cut short by a heart attack.

VIrgilio Afable—A physician-surgeon, he was the most sought-for doctor in Subic since before the war. "Mabait" (or good) was most people's word for him, and his emergence in later years as Zambales' congressman, after illustriously serving as director of the Olongapo General Hospital, summarily attests to this.

Aling Kanding Del Carmen Barquin—A dark-skinned woman, she is most particularly remembered for her heroic ways during the Japanese occupation of Subic. After her house got bombed (in Olongapo) by Japanese airplanes on December 8, 1941, she relocated to Subic—in a rented home in Calapandayan. There, she managed a general buy-and-sell business while maintaining her fishpond enterprise in Olongapo. Although she had a child to care for, she found herself a regular donor of food to guerrillas (some were Aetas) as well as a "trustee" of rifles issued and belonging to some of them. Also, she had gone out of her way to transport free up to twelve relatives from Cavite for economic relocation to Subic. "Whenever she received casual news from a Japanese soldier who was a past schoolteacher in his Japan hometown that 'barrio zoning' was scheduled to be held," narrates her only daughter, now Mrs. Josephina Bernal of Hayward, California, who once served as Miss Subic, "she would have the rifles under her care hidden up in coconut trees by a neighbor who was an expert climber."

Elsa Soriano Bitong—Neither political pull nor any other undue influence whatsoever played a role in her having attained the lofty position of vice-president of the PCI Bank. Instead, sheer workings of brain and uprightness constituted the steps of her stairway to it. Her intellect started budding even during her student days.

Huling Gallardo-Eclevia- She is one of the earliest Subiquenian emigrants to the US via marriage to Fred Eclevia who was employed in Guam in the 1950's. Like her husband, she is now a retired US naval base (Long Beach) employee—with great pride in having alll her three children (out of four) finished college, with one a cum laude and another still schooling. She owns two houses, with the other leased for side income. But she is most remembered for her great hospitality during fiestas, with relatives and friends flocking as guests to her family home in Calapandyan. She herself was once a popular fiesta queen, along with others serving also as such or damas (princesses) that included names like Ludy, Ester, Melicia, Nellie, Carmelita, etc.—in her own reminiscences. Love of family led her into fruitful immigrant visa petition of her only sister in Subic, Helding, along with the latter's husband, Tito Cruz.

Joe Emia—From his early employ as a bus driver who worked for the Victory Liner, he served and retired as one of Subic's municipal policemen from the 1950s to the 1970s. He belonged to one of Subic's ordinary families, yet earned the particular reputation of being looked up to as "defender of the physically disadvantaged." His robust build from adolescence to peak of adulthood combined to make him appear as if quite a formidable foe if anyone dared pick up a fist fight with him. But this tended not to be a motivation on his part, as otherwise was usually true of a bully. He was guided by his moral philosophy that reason rather than brawn ought to be the arbiter of any conflict that arises between a big guy and a small guy. People queued up at his funeral when he succumbed to diabetes.

Amelia Juico Gordon—Unknown to most Subiquenians, she was a native Subiquenian. Her becoming mayor of Olongapo City is in itself a sort of personal triumph over human nature's dark side that was responsible for the murder of her husband, Jimmy Gordon, Sr., of Castillejos, who became first elected mayor of Olongapo. But it is her having received the Pearl S. Buck International Award 2005 for her altruism as reflected in her humanitarian spirit for the care of orphan children that carries more meaning. Her civic work for Olongapo's Boys' Town has become virtually synonymous with her name. In the U.S., her counterpart was also a distinguished honoree and recipient of the award for 2006 is Laura Bush, wife of incumbent U.S. President George Bush.

Nene Juico—She was popularly known to most Subic folks from before the war up to the late 1970s. Although identified with one of Subic's old, name-prominent families, her popularity with people had to do more, however, with her famed neighborliness, a personal quality that had become synonymous with the common Tagalag word "mabait" (or "good"). By nature, she simply was friendly and not "mataas" (or "high-hat") to people, and it was for this reason, partly or wholly, that—even at middle age—she became the chosen bride of Alfredo ("Peding") Afable, who later became one of Subic's beloved mayors.

Ramon Lacbain III—His scholarly mettle as a Subicquenian saw him a topnotch elementary, then a secondary student. His greatest asset as such plus his humble but pervasive appeal among other youths of his generation proved to be such an endearment to them that he just got catapulted to Zambales' vice-governorship.

Juliet Soriano Lapason—As a product of the Philippine Normal College,

175

she is one of a few native Subiquenians who served as professional molders of grade school pupils in the Subic Central Elementary School until retirement. Her renowned amiability as an innate part of her dignified, almost criticism-free ways of dealing with people accounted for her being often designated master of ceremonies in almost every public social function held under the auspices of the municipal government, particularly during the administration of Mayor Dangal Guevara. She now lives in San Diego, California, with her husband, retired Dr. Melencio Lapazon.

Edwin Laroza—In search of greener pasture in Subic as a Batangueno professional civil engineer, he instead ended up marrying a street-corner rice retailer. When employed in the 1980s in the Subic municipal office, his wife was told of her being already on the way to becoming rich, in the wake of Edwin's being entrusted with an engineering position in government. But Edwin thought it wiser to cut short his tenure by outright resignation, rather than to stay put in his position via signing bills of construction materials showing anomalous pricings. His decision then saw him relegated to a much less prestigious—in fact, even a seemingly menial task of routinely carrying rice sacks over his shoulders, in conducting business. But some waiting eventually finds him now employed in the dignified practice of his engineering profession in California—the ultimate result of immigrant visa benefit realized via relative petition.

Leopoldo Lauzares—Although another Subiquenian who looks like a business tycoon-looking, he used to be fondly called "Mang Poldo" by most people. And it was the general aura of his naturally gracious personality that tended to make his town mates feel easily comfortable with their being with him anywhere. For this reason, partly or wholly, he easily became another beloved mayor of Subic. As such, it was apparently his good-heartedness that made him relieve a captured Japanese straggler from remaining hog-tied when brought to the old Subic municipal building in May 1945. One of his closest friends included Ramon Magsaysay, Sr., who later became one of the most beloved presidents of the Philippines.

Raymundo Lim—He started as a teacher in the Saint James High School in the 1960s. Now he is the principal of the Jesus Magsaysay High School in Mangan-Vaca, after a stint with a similar position in the Cawag High School. This may sound ordinary, for there are some others who have achieved a more or less similar professional stature as he. But he appears to most distinctively stand out, chiefly because to those who know him well, he is a paragon of matching his words with his deeds. His innate non-plasticity—the exact opposite of hypocrisy—is a factor in the government's choice for him to be the number-one public trustee of the educational molding of Subic's second-highest secondary school student enrolment: over 1,000.

Conrado Mercado—A pre-war migrant from Pampanga to Subic, he is the only teacher of the Subic Elementary School who became superintendent in the 1960s. After retirement, he served as one of the charter officers of the Subic Knights of Columbus in its founding in 1986. Not long thereafter, he served as president of the Subic Senior Citizens Association. Now in his 90s and a widower, he was married to the former Liwayway Deveraturda, who, as also a professional educator, was a retired principal of the Matain Elementary School. His being a career man with an unblemished record is what he is most reputedly known for.

Enrique Novales—Widely known to be one of Subic's successful MDs, Dr. Novales became particularly popular and identified with children patients. His reputation as being successful with children's ailments is such that patients are brought to his private clinic from places other than Subic. His having once an Olympic basketball player adds some weight to his fame, but it is actually his soft-spoken outlook, coupled with his dignified ways of living, that markedly accounts for his esteem.

Guillermo Pablo, Sr.—He was looked up to by many as one of the most respectable and reliable legal luminaries not only of Subic but also the whole of Zambales. It was his clean name and unstained reputation that greatly lent weight to his having become Justice of the Supreme Court of the Philippines.

Alfredo de Perio, Jr.—A native Subiquenian more popularly known as Fred or Junior, he remained one of the stellar mainstays of baseball in Subic. It was Olongapo City that found more use for him, however, in politics. As vice-mayor, he was a perennial political asset to whoever sat as city mayor. His name was never connected with graft and corruption, and he remained one of the steadfast advocates for all that the Knights of Columbus, the Catholic Church-connected fraternal organization, stands for.

Carmelita Custodio Pimentel—She graduated as high school valedictorian in 1950 and served as editor-in-chief of *The Bay*, the newspaper of the St. James High School. After becoming married to Atty. Marcial Pimentel, who became a Camarines Norte solon, inclination and talent saw her serving as music professor (voice culture) at Manila's Centro Escolar University. Relatives take extra pride over public acclaim for her professional expertise in concert music.

Antonio Quejado—He is well remembered particularly for his having proved a "Good Samaritan" during the Japanese occupation when a wound-nursing guerrilla, who was to later become president of the Philippines, Ferdinand E. Marcos, came to him for emergency health care. A brother of Luis Quejada, whose "parao" sea transport business helped many families in their evacuation and home relocations during Subic's occupation by the Japanese, Antonio had become Director of the Bureau of Forestry.

Evangeline Custodio Santiago—The youngest daughter of Ilwas' Felipe and Dominga Laag Custodio, she finished a Ph. D. in chemistry as a scholar in the University of the Philippines (UP). Currently serving as director of the UP Institute of Natural Science and Research, she is married to Felipe Santiago of Bulacan. She has a brother in San Jose, California, Joey Custodio, a past employee of the Subic Bay U.S. Naval Base and now an enthusiastic golf player.

Rosalinda De Perio Santos—She was a daughter of Jose De Perio, Sr., who was Subic's mayor from 1948-1951. Clean reputation, personality, education, and high-level connections collectively accounted for her enviable career in the Department of Foreign Affairs, where she served as ambassador to Geneva.

Severino Salang—He was an attorney-at-law whose parents reputedly first started with a successful "bagoong" or salted-fish-making business before ending up with the biggest textile business in Subic during the pre-war period. After serving as Subic mayor from 1944-1947, he got appointed in the 1960s to be head of the national government's Office of Economic Planning and Coordination. Although one of Subic's moneyed intellectuals, he nonetheless exhibits none of the so-called royal-blood ways of others who carry a white complexion, distinguishing Caucasian or European DNA in their veins. His down-to-earth, gracious dealings with people particularly account for his notability.

Lauro Simbol—Now on his third term as Subic vice-mayor, his popularity is pervasive among the masses but quite particularly with the young. Said to be given to being always generously open-palmed for reasonable causes, a personal asset customarily associated with most Filipinos' political fortunes, what is more deemed to be the primary reason for his staying power as an elective official, though, is his vaunted youthful charisma.

Rolando C. Young—Known to his contemporaries as a native Subiquenian domiciled in California, he is a child of parents with extensive, successful, businesses in Subic—Linga's grocery, lumber, hardware, gasoline, and banking. Amazingly these are not as impressive as his sense of values is. Rather than join them in business he had intimated his greater preference for staying put where he now resides in Bakersfield, in the company of his wife, Tess, and three children—Mickey, O'Niel, and Jill. Connected with California's Kern County Neurological Medical Group, Inc. as one of its doctors, Rolando has remained the same as how he used to be—naturally humble and unassuming, his relatively successful rise in his chosen profession notwithstanding.

APPENDIX A

Some Familiar Subic Bay U.S. Naval Base Workers Known to Have Gained Special Immigrant Visas for Creditable Service
(From both Subic Town and Olongapo City)

1. Sequel Albano
2. Moises Amith
3. Diego Arboleda (RIP)
4. Avel Bannag
5. Manny Bernal
6. Reuel Bundang
7. Joey Custodio
8. Bessie Carrero Cabal
9. Rudy Cabal
10. Ernie Casa
11. Ellen Casa
12. Joey Castillo
13. Ray Castillo
14. Leonardo Coronel
15. Lourdes Ednalino David
16. Jinny de Guzman
17. Ador Gorospe
18. Joe Gular
19. Manny Israel
20. Mar Labrador
21. Pepito Labrador
22. Dominador Medroso
23. Ben Mendoza
24. Lolita Mendoza
25. Angel Molina
26. Ida Molina
27. Virgie Custodio Molina
28. Art Padilla
29. Ligfino Raymundo
30. Myrla Raymundo
31. Manny Sapanlay

32. Tita Ammay Santos
33. Pres Soberon
34. Rey Victoria
35. Felix Villanueva
36. Olivo Yap
37. Linda Young

APPENDIX B

Subiquenians Known to Have Joined the U.S. Navy

PIONEER INDUCTEES (1945-1950):

1. Elio Del Carmen
2. Indo Custodio
3. Leonardo Custodio
4. Modesto Esteban
5. Marcelino Filamor
6. Alvaro Flores
7. Napoleon Flores
8. Peter Guerson
9. Joe Gonzales
10. Totoy Laborce
11. Fred Lopez
12. Domingo (Inggo) Martin
13. Memoy Mora (RIP)
14. Eding Pantaleon
15. Manuel Paulete
16. Apolonio Quejado, Jr.
17. David Servano
18. Pedro Tala
19. Democrito Tomilloso (RIP)
20. Teofilo Valdez (RIP)
21. Leonardo Custodio

LATER-PERIOD INDUCTEES:

1. Ricardo Amith
2. Rey Ammay
3. Rolando Bantugan
4. Bernard Baquir
5. Florante Beato
6. Jose Capati

7. Ceasar Custodio
8. Conrado Cusodo, Jr.
9. Duping Custodio
10. Moy Custodio
11. Pablo Custodio, Jr.
12. Robert Custodio
13. Andrew Dalopo
14. Ricky Dalopo
15. Simeon Ebue
16. Jing Eclar
17. Neptune Embat
18. Marcelo Esteban
19. Oscar Esteban
20. Sonny Esteban
21. Gil Fernandez
22. Gregorio Fontelera
23. Tonying Fortin (RIP)
24. Ganie Garcia
25. Rolando Gonzales
26. Arnulfo Huerta
27. Vic Huerta
28. Reden Infante
29. Ato Laag
30. Jesus Labampa
31. Lambert Labitan
32. Narding Ladao
33. Leonardo Lacbain
34. Jonathan Ligsay
35. Romeo Lim
36. August Lindawan
37. Totoy Lozano
38. Roque Macedo (RIP)
39. Phillip Magpoc
40. Tony Mamaril
41. Jose Galope Marquinez
42. Romualdes Galope Marquinez
43. Manuel Molina
44. Raul Molina

45. Frankie Del Monte
46. Marvin Del Monte
47. Jun Nepomuceno
48. Dionisio Ong
49. Robert Portacio
50. Wilfredo Portacio
51. Antonio Santa Presca (RIP)
52. Simeon Pullido
53. Roger Ramirez
54. Virgil Ramirez
55. Ato Ramos
56. Ed Ramos
57. Ceasar De La Rosa
58. Amor Del Rosario
59. Sen Viloria
60. Virgilio Viloria

APPENDIX C

Subiquenian Ladies Known to Have Married Incumbent or Past U.S. Navy Sailors

1. Erlinda Garcia Ammay
2. Cecilia (Celing) Salida Antonio
3. Corazon Valdez Arix
4. Elisea Soriano Bejasa
5. Yolanda Garcia Bantugan
6. Josephine (Pening) F. Bernal
7. Merle Tumaneng Clark
8. Dolly Apostol Cortez
9. Josie Custodio
10. Asuncion Francisco Dalopo
11. Susan Pagaduan Donovan
12. Analy (Lyn) Manalo Drumm
13. Carmen Pantaleon Ebue
14. Gerlie Lapazon Eclar
15. Juleta Eclar
16. Ludy Eugenio
17. Melicia (Meling) Roldan Eugenio
18. Regina Medroso Filamor
19. Pacita M. Flores
20. Zenaida Ponco Fontelera
21. Estella Ammay Gonzales
22. Gloria Romero Gonzales
23. Lota Custodio Greman
24. Binilda Santiago Holp
25. Zeny Francisco Huerta
26. Laarni Medroso Huerta
27. Princesita Embate Javier
28. Cristina (Neneng) Ramos de Jesus
29. Rene Lacbain
30. Puring Natividad Ladao
31. Aileen Antonio Libby
32. Claire Mendoza

33. Santa Mendoza
34. Del Ramirez Mora
35. Lilina Ordillas Nacario
36. Leonora Labrador Nimez
37. Cecilia (Diit) Ramos Pacoma
38. Dionisia Del Carmen Paulete
39. Milna N. de la Paz
40. Lanie Fernandez Santa Presca
41. Democrita Flores Shinn
42. Romelle Ladao Timones
43. Ela Fernadez Tinkham
44. Nellie Pagaduan Tucci

APPENDIX D

Respective Percentages of Subic's Eleven Ethnical Population Groups (Based on National Statistics Office's figures of 1955)

Ethnicity/Tongue Per Cent (of total population)

1. Bikol 0.62 %

2. Cebuano 2.36

3. Ilonggo 0.46

4. Ilokano 5.37

5. Kampampangan 1.82

6. Masbateno 0.38

7. Samal 0.88

8. Tagalog 82.88

9. Waray 1.28

10. Zambal 2.36

11. Others including Muslims 1.59

APPENDIX E

Educational Handout

How You as a Student Can Get High Grades in School

Ordinarily, getting high grades in school is deemed possible only for students born bright. But **any others with normalcy of ability, food, sleep, etc, can be as smart! Yes, you too can! How?** Here are 6-step acts you must do as a habit for your own stickler formula of success as a student. First, **be attentive—by all means**—to everything you do in class or as your teacher instructs. **Your attention is your primary pathway to your learning of school lessons. To learn is to understand, remember, or gain mastery of an idea, skill, attitude, talent, method, or procedure essential to education that we all need to get—if we are at all to enhance our usefulness to ourselves, family, or society—even to all humanity.**

Second, you'd do well accepting the fact that while **life is God-given, education is not, so we have to acquire it in order to go on with life assured of a worthy future: our enhanced worthiness as described above. Anyone can carry on with life uneducated, but this is like possessing an irreplaceable gift, yet lacking knowledge of how best to use and enjoy it for all its worth.**

Third, remember that **learning is a function and domain only of our brain, and it becomes effective only if our attention is not disrupted but on focus. Our attentiveness is our brain's connection to knowledge flow and if it is disrupted or disconnected, knowledge will not flow into our head.** This is by the same token that an electric bulb darkens once disconnected—because of stoppage of electricity flow into it. In another sense, **good learning occurs only where there's good teaching. But this is true only when our brain intently maintains in class good attention, not its disconnection.**

Fourth, **for better learning, ask your teacher for further explanations as needed, take down notes, make diagrams, or do any other things you think will enable you to get a better grasp of problematic lessons.** If you're learning math, self-drill on solving problems is a "must" for you to do. If it is science or language arts, **you need to do a lot of reading, thinking, memorizing, and note-taking. An additional insurance for your better** learning is a pocket dictionary. **It facilitates your vocabulary enrichment—a vital key to cultivating your interest in your studies, because adequacy in your knowledge of words is what would best sustain your being always connected with the myriad challenges facing you as a student.**

Fifth, be sure **the friends you keep are obedient to school rules and enjoy more fun doing assignments during breaks, rather than listening to school-prohibited electronic devices.**

Lastly, think: You're now in school **to harness your own brain potential and power to achieve ultimately your own dreamed-of future in life—with your character or kind of heart as your primordial guide.** If you dream of a high-paying job, then a 4-year college degree is a "must." By it you can earn $1,920,000.00 after 40 years, at an average pay of $48,000.00/yr. (or $4,000.00/mo.), computed thus: 40 yrs. x $48,000.00/yr. = $1,920,000.00. If you divide $1,920,000.00 by the total number of hours required for your full schooling from kindergarten to college—which totals 18,360 hours (based on 1 yr. kindergarten + 6 yrs. elementary + 2 yrs. junior high school + 4 yrs. senior high school = 17 school years; 17 sc. yrs. times 180 days/sc. yr. = 3,060 sc. days; and 3,060 sc. days x 6 hrs. /sc. day = 18,360 hrs.), the resulting quotient is $105.00/hr. (rounded to nearest dollar). This represents what you, in effect, earn—for your future—every hour that you learn from your work in school (supposedly out of a total of 18,360 learning hours)—or lose forever if you're not learning at all! How you lose it is answerable by the fact that before you can land a job paying $4,000.00/mo. or $48,000.00/yr., (more in certain cases), you need to pass a test for it—and **only what your brain is now telling you to do in school could make you pass—and get the high-paying job! High-level attention in school makes for high grades, so high achievers enjoy higher chances of high income later on.**

APPENDIX F

Student-Faculty Population and Administrators of Schools in Subic, as of January 2007 (Compiled by the Subic Department of Education District Office)

School	Students	Teachers	Name of Administrator
Public Elementary:			
Agusuhin E.S.	179	3	Fernando F. Felarca, Head Teacher I
Aning.-Sacatihan E.S.	192	10	Maria Leticia A. Menorca, Head Teacher III
Batiawan E.S., Annex I	37	3	Macario S. Sahagun, Principal II
Batiawan E.S., Main	77	3	Macario S. Sahagun, Principal II
Batiawan E.S., Annex II	73	2	Macario S. Sahagun, Principal II
Cabitaugan E.S.	216	5	Aurora F. De Luna, Teacher-in-Charge
Calapacuan E.S.	1,206	32	Elena J. Sahagun, Principal I
Calapandayan E.S.	946	24	Lerma Aranas, Head Teacher I
Cawag E.S.	89	2	Amena M. Duque, Teacher-in-Charge
Cawag Resettlement	129	4	Alvin G. Apdal, Teacher-in-Charge
Ilwas E.S.	644	17	Merlina P. Cruz, Ph.D., Principal I
Josephine F. Khong for the Gifted	130	7	
Kinabukasan E.S.	101	5	Angelito C. Sinfuego, Head Teacher
Manggahan E.S.	609	16	Deudeline P. Damondon, Principal I
Mapanao P. S.	25	2	Annabel Cielo, Teacher-in-Charge
Matain E.S.	1,835	46	Macario S. Sahagun, Principal II
Nagyantok E.S.	153	3	Elvira S. Pantorgo, Teacher-in-Charge
Naugsol E.S.	117	6	Isidro Matute, Principal I
Pamatawan E.S.	366	12	Edwin E. Ventura
San Isidro E.S.	696	17	Isidro Matute, Principal I
Santo Tomas E.S.	457	15	Lilia B. Rosete, Principal I
Subic Central School	2,022	55	Rogelio T. Encarnacion, Principal II
Tibag E.S.	54	2	Isidro Matute, Principal I

Public High School:

Cawag Resetlement H.S.	129	5	Romero Fastidio, Officer-in-Charge
Cawag H.S., Annex	207	3	Jane Jose, Officer-in-Charge
Jesus Magsaysay H.S.	1,077	29	Raymundo V. Lim, Principal I
Subic National H.S.	1,943	62	Felita Pullido, Ed. D., Principal II

Private High School:

Saint James School	900	32	Sr. Rosa C. Mendoza, Principal
Saint Anthony H.S.	519	29	Isabelita Hipolito, Principal

Private School:

Saint Anne E.S.	N. A.	N. A.	Unavailable
Subic Montessori	114	28	Orlinda Bertrame
Smart Kids	94	5	Editha De Guzman

College:

Kolehiyo ng Subic	1,075	58	Jeffrey D. Khonghun, President

Subic Department of Education District Supervisor: Amelia H. Mojica, Ed. D.

APPENDIX G

St. James School Alumni Reunion '05 and 60th Anniversary Celebration*
Suncoast Hotel & Casino, Las Vegas Nevada, July 23, 2005
(Jointly coordinated by alumni committee members & Subic Association of San Diego)

Class Year	Alumni Reunion Committee Member
1950	Moy Ebue
1962	Andy Dalopo
1962	Cesar Del Rosario
1963	Phillip Magpoc
1963	Willie Portacio
1963	Ricardo Soriano
1964	Priscilla Embate Portacio
1965	Ganie Garcia
1965	Jun Nepomuceno
1965	Myrna Garcia Soriano
1966	Lynn Ordillas Nacario
1967	Junie Esteban
1971	Rita Flores Shinn
1972	Gerlie Lapazon Eclar
1972	Jing Eclar
1973	Amor Del Rosario
1973	Aileen Antonio Libby
1974	Gerry Vindua
1976	Tessi Nepomuceno Anicete
1977	Beng Decusar Guizom
1979	Malou Fontelera Bartlett
1979	Manolo Lapazon

Milna De La Paz—Treasurer
Elvie Canlas Del Rosario—Asst. Treasurer

Officers Representing Subic Association of San Diego   Position in Association

Andy Dalopo   President
Aileen Antonio Libby and Malou Fontelera Bartlett   Vice Presidents
Gerlie Lapazon Eclar andMyrna Garcia Soriano   Secretaries
Milna De La Paz Freedman and Elvie Canlas Del Rosario   Treasurers
Amor Del Rosario and Jojo Esteban   Business Managers
Rita Flores Shinn   Auditor
Bing Decusar Guimzon   Public Relations Officer
Cesar Del Rosario and Manolo Lapazon Sergeants-at-Arms
Lynn Ordillas Nacario, Ric Soriano, Junie Esteban   Directors
Simeon Ebue, and Beth Garcia De La Paz
   * List comes from the affair's souvenir program hand-outs for attendees.

APPENDIX H

Spanish Infantry Captain's Letter-Report on Aetas' Raid on Subic in 1892
(Addressed to governor of Zambales of the time)

Your Excellency:

From a report I received from the Mayor of the Town of Subic and the Visita of Ugvit within the jurisdiction of this office, it is very obvious how much grief there was on the days of the 8th, the 13th, and the 16th of the current month when the Negritos of the mountain attacked several natives of the said town, resulting in the wounding of three individuals and the killing of two. With such disaster and fatal events, the natives are submerged in great consternation, and they are possessed with panicky terror that prevents them from going out of their houses to devote themselves to the chores of their farms, cutting wood, rattan, and others which essentially constitute their daily subsistence. Consequently, the town Mayor and the community folks informed (and asked me) personally, in the name of the town, to enter the mountains which border with them, with the aim of repelling and containing the boldness of those erring men and mountain people and who, on the other hand, are cowards and even treacherous, considering that they can cause irreparable damage or harm to the rest of the province. It appears proper to me to bring this to Your Excellency's knowledge, so that in your outlook, you may consider opportune to bring about the particulars; and it is my idea that in case Your Excellency may accede to the means of prosecuting the perpetrators, it should be extended to all the towns of this province, executing so simultaneously in Pangasinan, Pampanga and Bataan; where and when they cannot be subjected in the manner proposed, gather and make them stay together in the neighboring towns recognizing the government, or they must desist from their bloody undertaking, since by indifferently looking at their actions, which curtail the development of agriculture and commerce, it will fill those barbarians with pride, tending to make them go on with their offensive practices at frequencies more and more alarming to peaceful inhabitants.

I wish God grant Your Excellency more years,
Royal House of Iba, May 28, 1892,
Manuel Yparraguirre

APPENDIX I

Zambales Governor's Letter-Report on Typhoon's Havoc on Subic in 1850 (Addressed to the Spanish governor-general of the Philippines at the time)

His Excellency:

The unexpected typhoon on the 5th day of the current month that passed the country without having done damages to this province but in the last town on the south, which is Subic, made the mayor inform the Provincial Governor of the following misfortunes:
The first one, demolition of forty-two houses in the Poblacion, the front of its church, and deterioration of the parochial houses and tribunal; and the second, breakdown of the floors of thirty houses inside the town, and de-roofing of all of the rest of them including the tribunal, the convent, and the church where some lumbers of their walls were destroyed, along with several posts of the place in which they stood; and this is not what is most terrible but the extraordinary inundation which they suffered during the typhoon. On the morning of these calamities, the town mayor of Subic also reported the arrival in the Cove of Cabitaogan of the schooner No. 7 Bosearena, owned by Don Francisco Placido Orbeta, with a cargo of tobacco in bundles; the destruction of the rudder, foresails, and all other sails of a Parao that sunk in the island, whose owner Don Jose Rios and five individuals of the crew, presented themselves before him, including also the skipper of the Parao Santa Catalina of Dona Isabel del Fierro, which sunk in the inlet of Silangin with a cargo of rice, all of which are now here brought to the knowledge of that authority. I want to point out that I have ordered remedy of the damages.

I wish God help Your Excellency,
Iba, May 18, 1850,
Jose Sanchez Guerrero

Bibliography

Anderson, Gerald R. *History of Subic Bay*, Internet-available publication, 2006

Dimalanta, Esther F., Mercado, Lino F., and Solomon, Lydia E. *Subic Through the Years* (research book project sponsorship and funded by the Subic municipal government,
Olongapo City: Aaron's Press, 1998)

Dolan, Ronald E., ed. *Philippines: A Country Study*, 4th ed., Washington, DC: GPO for
the Library of Congress, 1993

New Standard Encyclopedia, Standard Educational Corporation, Chicago, 1981

Saint James School Souvenir Program (public handout), 60th Anniversary Celebration,
Sun Coast Hotel & Casino, Las Vegas, Nevada, July 23, 2005

Thomasites—Wikipedia, the free encyclopedia; information from Answers.com; and
Before and After, Internet-available referential information

Subic Municipal Building as modernized in 2003

Subic poblacion's main street as of 2005

Subic Public Market's "bulungan" or (whispered bidding) building

The Subic Shipyard & Engineering, Inc. (formerly PHILSECO) seen from the sea

Jesus F. Magsaysay High School

Front view of the Club Morocco Hotel

The Sneak Island

White Rock Hotel viewed from the sea

White Rock Beach Resort

Cawag site for the HANJIN Heavy Industries for shipbuilding

Partial view of Cawag, Subic's largest barangay

Calapacuan communications facilities

Shoreline leading to Subic Public Market's whispered bidding building

Atin Beach Resort

Old Subic Muncipal Building believed constructed in 1910

New Subic Municipal Building (renovated in 2003 into the now modern building with complete air-con units)